Brown Girl in the Ring

PLAYS, PROSE AND POEMS

by

Valerie Mason-John

aka

QUEENIE

Get A Grip

London

First published in 1999 by Get A Grip Publishers Ltd
The Master's House, The Old Lambeth Workhouse, off Renfrew Road, London SE11 4TH

British Library Cataloguing Publication Data. A catalogue record for this book is available
from the British Library.

ISBN 0-9525789-1-3

Distributed by :
Turnaround, Unit 3, Olympia Trading Estate, Coburg Road, London N22 6TZ (UK).
Alamo Square Distributors, PO Box 14543, San Francisco, CA 94114 (USA).

This edition is printed on acid-free paper.

Typeset, printed and bound by 'The Oval Printshop', London (UK).

Cover photograph by Vanda Playford.
Cover design by 'The Oval Printshop', London (UK).

I dedicate this book to my foster mother,
CAROL ANN GALLAGHAR.

Without you I don't know if I would have survived.
Thank you for loving me, trusting in me and at a later date
sharing your new family with me – my foster father, Bob Piggot,
and three foster sisters, Emma, Rebecca and Sarah.

May they in their lives, along with the many children you take
care of through your courageous work as a Guardian Ad-Litem,
reap the benefits of your stamina and sensitivity.

ACKNOWLEDGEMENTS

My thanks are too numerous to list every person who has supported me and believed in my work. So I take this opportunity to thank all the people who have read my other books, come along to my shows and visited my nightclub, 'Queenies', at The Fridge, Brixton.

There are people I want to thank more specifically. Mita Datta, who read my work diligently and gave me constructive feedback and support. Steve Cranfield and Martin Humphries for their enthusiasm and faith in the book. Strawb for taking time out of her hectic schedule to add the finishing touches to the front cover. To my beloved friend, Jo Fraser-Odin, for her continued support and encouragement and for keeping me up to date with what the black media are saying about me. Jennifer Dean for her belief in my work, her love and financial support for my theatre projects. To Jackie, Marge, Harriet and Lorna for standing beside me and watching me grow throughout the years. To my children's home family, Shirley, Kevin, Janet, Donald, Shanel, Trini and Rhyss. Paul Everitt for his belief in my creative work and my co-director of Pride Arts Festival, Tom Brooks, for his support. Punyvati, Moksanandi, Sobhana and Vimlacitta for supporting me in my spiritual practice. Thank you to Alan and Roberta at 'The Oval Printshop' who suggested Get A Grip might be interested in this book. Thank you for the regular support of my Mitra Study Group, Zenobi, Ali, Ginny, Robyn, Tricia and Diane. Thank you to the good witches of the Tangled Roots group for brewing their loving potions.

The poems 'The Colour of My Skin' and 'Tangled Roots' are part of a permanent art installation designed by Veena Stephenson for an African-Caribbean and Asian housing headquarters, Unity, in Chapeltown, Leeds. 'The Colour of My Skin' was later included in an anthology published by the Centreprise Project in London.

Finally I would like to thank one of my heroines, Linda Bellos, who was witch-hunted throughout her time as Leader of Lambeth Council for being lesbian, black, Jewish and a mother. Thank you for your courage, strength and authenticity. It is an inspiration.

CONTENTS

INTRODUCTION _page_ 1

References 7

SECTION ONE – MY AWAKENING TO LESBIANISM 8

SECTION TWO – PUBLISHED AND BE DAMNED

Black – Part of a Lesbian Identity 11

The Scene: Part of a Black Lesbian Identity 15

Coming Out 19

Luv Up White Gal Dem 22

Luv Up Black Gal 28

P.C. Definitions 30

Dyke Spotting 35

References 40

SECTION THREE – SIN DYKES

The Play: Sin Dykes 41

SECTION FOUR – QUEENIE COMES TO TOWN

Born to Be a Queen 91

Inglan Is a Bitch 92

Brown Girl in the Ring 99

Black Taboos 113

Please God 116

SECTION FIVE – CONFUSED? CELIBATE? LESBIAN? 120

INTRODUCTION

This collection of prose, poetry, monologues and a play documents some of my experiences from the mid-1980s to the late 1990s, through the eyes of a diva, a dyke, a scene gal, a raver, a black woman living in London. '*Brown Girl in the Ring*' is a book about everything I really wanted to say in my first two books, but censored myself because it was more important that both African and Asian lesbians had a book that belonged to them, and could even buy one for their relatives or close heterosexual friends if they had the courage to do so. '*Brown Girl in the Ring*' is my story about being black, woman and lesbian in Britain, told through prose, poetry, drama and story telling. It fuses fiction, fact and fantasy to offer a rich multi-layered narrative. It's not a conventional way of telling a story and it doesn't slot things into neatly labelled compartments, either. Each section has its own angle which builds up to create a whole 'story' about a brown girl once ring-fenced by lesbian culture, sexuality, racism and oppression. As a woman of African descent, born in Britain, and transracially placed in Barnardo's and foster homes, I can only really write from my own perspective ... while I refer to the experience of other black women, it is only in reference to my immediate experience.

* * *

'*Brown Girl in the Ring*' completes a trilogy of works documenting the lives of African, Caribbean and Asian women who have contributed to black, lesbian and women's culture in Britain.

In my first book '*Making Black Waves*' (Scarlet Press, 1993), I invited the Asian lesbian, activist and writer Ann Khambatta to join me in documenting part of African, Caribbean, and Asian women's culture in Britain. It was the first to record black lesbian history in this country and to discuss some of the issues that affected our lives during the late 70s and 80s.

In my second book '*Talking Black: African and Asian Lesbians Speak Out*' (Cassell, 1995), I commissioned (as editor) ten writers/political activists/educators to be part of the first black British lesbian anthology. It explored politics, discrimination, mental health, sexuality, age, literature, film and history.

This book caused a furore in the media after the London based listings magazine *Time Out* printed an article in its lesbian and gay pages. Black and white members of the lesbian community came together in outrage against what struck us and many others as the blatant racism of the article. The Lesbian Avengers zapped the magazine's London offices, and I took the publication to the Press Complaints Commission. *Time Out* received many letters and telephone calls of complaint. In the end they printed an edited version of my letter along with others on their letters page. After much deliberation, the Press Complaints Commission decided not to take the matter further, as I had been given right of reply by the offending magazine.

Such a public attack from part of the white lesbian community, coupled by an attack from part of the black lesbian thought police (several years earlier) against me and another black woman for "seeming to have special favours from white women", told me it was time to get out of the ghetto and live.

Once I realised that what I had to say didn't fit into the comfortable niche of black, lesbian and feminist, it gave me the courage to say what I wanted without fear of criticism. After all, my nearest and dearest siblings, black and white lesbians, had already tried to tear me apart and I survived to tell the tale.

'*Brown Girl in the Ring*' completes my series on the contribution of African, Caribbean and Asian lesbian culture to the lesbian and gay world, the black world and the mainstream. It is also my transition from the populist confining world of journalism, which I once belonged to, to the artistic world of performance, poetry and theatre.

* * *

Just in case you're wondering what all this black lesbian stuff is about, or thinking it can't possibly happen in your country of origin, for the record:

MYTH

Homosexuality is a white, male, upper class, able-bodied disease found in the West. If homosexuality is found anywhere else, it is a result of colonisation.

FACTS

"Lesbian bonding by African women does herstorically exist. Lesbian relationships are recognised as legitimate social relationships in certain African societies." [1]

"In Nigeria marrying women is old. It is bush ways." [2]

"Where I come from (Barbados) we use the term wicka. It means women who love women." [3]

"Zami: Another Spelling of My Name." [4]

"There are, always have been, and always will be lesbians in India. In fact we have quite a long rich history and tradition of lesbianism and homosexuality." [5]

"If you look at early Hindu scripture and culture you will find a lot of homosexuality suppressed by British culture." [6]

"In 500 AD writers described harems as 'hotbeds' of lesbianism." [7]

* * *

As a lesbian of African descent living in the West during the 20th century, I have been affected at times by people of African, African-Caribbean and Asian descent stating that homosexuality, lesbianism and feminism are 'white diseases', phenomena of white Western culture. I have at times asked myself:

- If Africa and the Caribbean had not been colonised, would I be heterosexual?

- If my ancestors had not been displaced, scattered in the West, and the Caribbean, creating the African Diaspora, would I have been heterosexual?

- If I had not been transracially placed as a baby in white institutions and with white families, would I be heterosexual?

It wasn't until I had discovered that women loving women sexually and emotionally was part of African and African-Caribbean cultures, that I could really begin to feel whole as a woman of African descent. I could acknowledge that if lesbianism and homosexuality were phenomena of Western culture, there would not be words in African, Caribbean and Asian languages or evidence of homosexual societies in places where black women in Britain originate.

Co-writing the first book on African and Asian lesbians in Britain, 'Making Black Waves', was a healing, affirming, and exciting process for me. However, I admit I have to accept that perhaps the way I live my life, as a woman of African descent who is a lesbian in the West, would be very different if I was living back home in Africa. It is likely that I would not be rich enough to buy a woman and set up home with her, rearing our children together like some of the wealthy women in Kenya from the Kuriar tribe, or Nigerian women from the Yoruba, Akoko and many other tribes.[8] Most women in Africa are dependent on men for economic survival, and therefore cannot become financially independent. However, in these circumstances, I could still enjoy sexual, intimate relationships with other women whilst living in a conventional heterosexual institution.

* * *

WHAT'S IN THE BOOK?

My Awakening To Lesbianism contextualises who I am, what shaped me before defining myself by my colour or who I slept with.

Publish and Be Damned explores the ring of lesbian culture, politics, definitions, and oppressions which have shaped many of us on the political and social scene of the 80s and 90s.

Sin Dykes explores the ring of lesbian sexuality, black and white, touching on the taboos of all black-white relationships in everyday culture and sado-masochistic sex. When this play was first written I was told it was ahead of its time. First staged in 1998, it was a box office sell out, and members from all sections of society flocked to see it. I would not have had the courage to write this play five years earlier because of the confining political and social arena that I was then part of. It also challenges the notion that black writers can only write for and about black characters.

Queenie Comes to Town includes a comedy monologue which explores the scenarios of black people growing up in Britain. In it I imagine myself as a throwback in a family of white people spanning five generations. It touches on what many of us experience daily: the effects of racist assumptions, fears and ignorance, expressed consciously and unconsciously in thought and behaviour. This section also explores the rings we as black people have put around ourselves, and touches on the taboo of abuse towards each other.

'Brown Girl in the Ring' ends where it begins. Now awakened to lesbian culture, I am a *Confused? Celibate? Lesbian?* living in the 90s. Say no more.

AFRICAN PRINTS

I have existed in Africa, Asia, the Caribbean Islands, Indigenous Australasia and the Americas before my lands were ever colonised by the West. I am African, I am Nubian, I am Woman, I am Lesbian, born in Britain.

Nubian woman
Asian woman
Latino woman
Mediterranean woman
Caucasian woman
African woman

I come to you
In African prints
Robed in Kentae
Swamped
Wrap after wrap
Kaftan over kaftan
Sari around saris.

I am your dark knight
Nubian Queen
Mounted between your strong sturdy thighs
Trickling down your soft, ebony, ivory skin
My dew caramelising on chocolate fudge
Sticky toffee crystalline on tips of fingers

I come to you in thunder and lightening
Flashes of
Red Blacks
Blue Blacks
Black Blacks

Streaks of
Browns
Reds
Caramels
Mochas.

I am your illusion
Swallowed by thoughts
Consumed by fantasies
And as I kiss your body
I surrender to you

Foraging through your forest
Of
afros
kinks
braids
crew cuts
dredloks
bobs
cane row
ringlets
china bumps
twists
waves
threads

Gyroscoping in illuminating awareness

I know this is
Nubian woman
Asian woman
Latino woman
Mediterranean woman
Caucasian woman
African woman

REFERENCES

1) Vickie M Mays, 'I hear voices but see no faces. Reflections on racism and woman-identified relationships of Afro-American Women', published paper, US, 1981

2) V Mason-John and A Khambatta (eds), *Making Black Waves* (Lesbians Talk Series) Scarlet Press, original source interviewee, Femi Otitoju, 1993

3) Ibid., original source interviewee, Marie

4) Audre Lorde, *Zami: A New Spelling of My Name*, Persephone Press, Watertown, Massachussets, 1982

5) Radio interview aired on WBAI, New York City, April 29, 1984

6) V Mason-John and A Khambatta (eds), op. cit., original source interviewee, Linda Bellos

7) Ibid.

8) Ibid., original source *Cosmopolitan*

SECTION ONE

MY AWAKENING TO LESBIANISM

Seven years old, walking arm in arm with my best friend Ann across the football green in my children's home village, some boys from a nearby town, who were passing through, yelled out: Are you lesbians? Ann and I held onto each other's arms tightly, and proudly shouted back, No we're tomboys, and merrily skipped off home together.

I'm eight years old, sitting at a dining room table, eating family dinner. Children should be seen and not heard, was the Victorian motto. So I listened, especially after returning from our annual Summer Holiday. The adults always had interesting anecdotes to tell. Today, it was the one about women who liked using male toilets. One of the teenage boys living in my cottage reported back that he had gone to use the public toilet and saw women who looked like men, wearing Y-fronts. So naturally, for the next eight years I thought lesbians were women who wore Y-fronts and used only male toilets. After all these years, I'm still trying to work out how he managed to see their underwear.

During this same summer, one of the bad boys who lived outside of the village was in the neighbourhood. I'm happily playing on my bike outside my cottage. He comes up to me and tells me to cycle over to the long grass behind the hospital, and wait for him. I'm scared, but like a good little girl I do as I'm told. I wait for him. When he arrives, he pushes me to the ground. He pulls my knickers down, and tries ramming his penis inside me. I manage to resist his penis, I scream inside my head, I never want this thing near me again.

Aged 9, my biological mother begins to make spasmodic contact, I begin going home to her for the odd weekend. On one occasion, whilst having to watch her cook, I verbally announce how bored I am, and openly pine for my friends. She asks me who I play with and what do we do? I innocently reply: "Climb trees, play conkers, build camps, play football. Play with Ann, Marjorie, Kevin, Paul, Stuart." She stops me in mid-flow, and asks me if I would like to be a boy. I innocently answer Yes. After all, they are allowed to play and get their clothes dirty. She throws a carving knife at me, I duck, it hits the wall, she beats me. I don't understand what's wrong with wanting to be a boy, but I realise some people are upset by this.

Aged 11, forced to return to my biological mother. It is the era of trying to reunite children in orphanages with their parents if they can be found. I am my biological mother's worst nightmare. A white English child inside a coal black skin. She tries to beat the white out of me. She sadistically tortures and abuses me. Her mental health is obviously disturbed.

Aged 12 and a half, I am taken back into care, my school have reported to the police finding visible bruises on my body. My biological mother is taken to court and I am made a Ward of Court.

I return back to my children's home village, and attend the local grammar school. I become obsessed with a girl sitting in front of me. She is my complete opposite, white, quiet, timid and shy. I dream about her, and even have the courage to tell her. She laughs because my dream of her having her hair cut was true.

One night I lie awake, with my head full of thoughts about her. I'm obsessed, I feel this emotion which I think is love. I panic, and begin praying to God: "Please God stop me thinking such evil thoughts." I prayed every night for a week, until the corrupt work of Satan had completely disappeared.

That same year, I'm hanging out with my school friends in our registration class. We're joking, gossiping about the weekend. I stick my tongue out, my friends squeal. I laugh and say: "You know what that's good for?" In unison they ask: "What for?" I reply: "For licking the girls out with." I don't know where that thought came from, but it was most definitely uttered. Of course, my class mates scream with disgust.

Aged 15, I'm remanded in custody at Holloway prison. My crime, living in a children's home, a runaway, and a shoplifter. Six months later, my case is heard at crown court, my social worker recommends borstal. A month later, I'm shipped out of Holloway to a closed borstal. The first day I arrive I see young women walking round, with love bites all over their necks. I am horrified.

One day I walk into the television room, I stop at the doorway, with horror I witness several women rape one woman with a broomstick and deodorant bottle. I'm devastated, shell shocked, the screws pay no attention, I feel sick inside. I had to acknowledge women could be just like men.

I'm 17, it's my last goddam night in borstal, a screw unlocks my cell, she has come to say goodbye, whispering her address into my ear. She hugs me, walks out banging the door behind her, and locking me up for the last time. My fellow inmates give me a traditional farewell sing-out through the windows at night, and at breakfast in the morning.

I collect my belongings, my peers and screws say goodbye, sincerely wishing me well, I sit in a van, and look ahead, I'm travelling towards my future lover.

I know I love this woman, but I'm not sure how, loving her like a mother feels definitely wrong, but it's the only acceptable definition I know of, for loving another woman. And what would I do with her in bed?

On my eighteenth birthday, my hymen is broken, I bleed a little on her sheets. I enter the mysterious world of adulthood. I loved to madness, I am Thomas Hardy's heroine, Eustacia, from his book *Return of the Native*.

Seventeen years my senior, married, and a mother, I moved into her marital home. Only four years later, when this relationship was over, did I really begin to discover what a lesbian was. When I plucked up the courage to tell my foster mother why I had left home to live with a woman, she said, maybe you'll meet a nice young man now. I knew she was wrong. But, she was right in saying at least I had learned to love.

SECTION TWO

PUBLISH AND BE DAMNED

BLACK: PART OF A LESBIAN IDENTITY

TANGLED ROOT

Tangled to life's roots
Rooted to life's tangles
Tangling to manmade ways
Rooting to life's decay
New roots grow
New tangles show
My roots are tangling
My tangles are rooting
I am the tangled root

In Britain, black in the political arena is often defined as those "descended (through one or both parents) from Africa, Asia (i.e. the Middle East to China, including the Pacific nations), and Latin America, and those descended from the original inhabitants of Australasia, North America, and the islands of the Atlantic and Indian Ocean." [1]

Many people from the US ask why does black include those who are not of African descent? Our history as black people living in the British diaspora is different. The first recorded evidence of Africans and Asians born in Britain dates back to 1505. (However, the earliest attested dated for Africans in Britain is the year 210: an African soldier.) During the seventeenth and eighteenth centuries young African and Asians were brought to Britain to work as domestic slaves. [2]

We were all wogs, all niggers, all coons. As a young child growing up in the country, I was called coloured along with children of Indian, Pakistani, Chinese, and Japanese descent, and any one else who didn't resemble white. Immigration laws were made specifically to keep the 'West Indians', Africans, Indians and Pakistanis out of

Britain. For example, in 1962 a law was passed to restrict the entry of immigrants into Britain. In response, organisations like the Federation of the Coloured People's Progressive Association were set up, which included Africans, Caribbeans and Asians.

I only became aware of our differences while reading Politics and Philosophy at Leeds University. I was told by an Asian woman from Kenya I was inferior to her because I was black. This was my rude awakening to the fact that we were not all one homogeneous group, as racism had led me to believe.

People of African, Caribbean and Asian descent living in Britain were called coloured right up to the 80s, and still are, outside of the major cities. However, the Civil Rights and Black Power movements in America made the term 'black' popular as a political label for people to adopt in Britain. Black became an umbrella term for political organisations. In 1962 the National Black People's Alliance was set up. This organisation included the Federation of Pakistani Associations, Universal Coloured Peoples Association, West Indian Standing Conference, and the Indian Workers Conference. Groups like these recognised our common oppression against colonialism and imperialism in our countries of origin.

Many lesbians of African, Caribbean and Asian descent born in Britain or who settled in Britain during the 60s can recall being labelled black. "In 1964 I arrived in England with my immediate family (from Sri Lanka). We were most definitely categorised as black by the state, and by white British people," writes Savitri Hensman. [3]

"Black is a very British term, and if you've just come from India, nobody tells you at the airport you're now supposed to call yourself black." [4]

"The first time I realised I was black was when I came to England, In Jamaica being black wasn't an issue." [5]

British culture has tried very hard to homogenise Africans, Caribbeans and Asians by calling us immigrants, foreigners, coloureds and blacks, to the extent that there has been confusion to who is or isn't black in our own communities.

During the 70s it seemed quite clear that women of African, Caribbean and Asian descent were black. The black political movements had brought black women together in one space. Let down by the global black struggle, women set up the first and only black national political women's organisation in Britain, the Organisation of Women of Africa and African Descent (OWAAD) in 1978. "However, during its first year it was argued that if OWAAD was to address issues concerning all black women effectively, women of African and Asian descent should stop organising separately." [6] A year later, the name changed to the Organisation of Women of African and Asian descent, uniting black women throughout Britain.

Sadly, this organisation collapsed in 1982. However, its demise was significant for black lesbians defining themselves in public for the first time and hence, for the formation of the first black lesbian group, Brixton Black Lesbian Group. Throughout the 60s and 70s black lesbians had played a significant part in the Black Power and Civil Rights movements, but had remained invisible through fear.

Coming together as black women, it felt like a safe place for some women to identify as black lesbians. One brave woman at an OWAAD conference announced that there was no space for a black lesbian workshop, "So let's have it over here." Insults and abuse were hurled at her. How, it was argued, could black women waste time debating issues of lesbianism, bisexuality and heterosexism when there were more pressing issues. [7]

In 1982, Brixton Black Lesbian Group was founded, and catered for women throughout England and Scotland. This group, predominantly attended by women of African descent, was also the subtle beginning of some black women redefining black for themselves. OWAAD's collapse was also triggered by the fact that there were many individuals and groups of women who did not feel united under the black banner, although in theory the cry for unity among Africans, Caribbeans and Asians was intellectually recognised.

Inevitably a fundamental part of black lesbians defining ourselves has been around our racial identity, because of living in a country where we have been oppressed. This has lead to painful debates around who is or not black, to the extent that we have at times imposed self-apartheid upon our own communities.

Some respondents to a questionnaire for my first book 'Making Black Waves', wrote:

"I have been called half breed in some black women's groups."

"As I look light I'm not readily accepted by the black lesbian community."

"I've been called a black slut, I've been called a white slut, I've been called a half-black slut, I've been called a half-white slut."

"Groups might say black means ... and use some exact definition, but inevitably when I got to the door, I'd always be checked out. I had to end up giving a potted family history."

Because the term black has been an integral part of our identity for many black lesbians, the definition has caused some problems. When black lesbians have come together and organised their own parties, conferences, workshops, and clubs, some women have been turned away because their skin colour has not been dark enough. The excuse is that they resemble 'white' lesbians. However, there are some lesbians of African descent who have covertly held on to the view that black means of African and African-Caribbean descent.

One Asian lesbian I interviewed said: "I have become more wary of calling myself black, because of the truths I can omit around skin privilege."

This misunderstanding around the definition of black has led some black lesbians to adopt the American term 'of colour.'

"I love the term 'of colour'. That describes me. Black events are inevitably mainly Afro-Caribbean." [8]

Although the term 'of colour' has broadened the definition of who is black in terms of skin colour, it has not provided a solution to the difficulties in defining a black lesbian or community. 'Of colour' has the horrible reminder of being called the 'coloured people', a term which was commonly used to describe us.

I believe part of the solution could be achieved by defining ourselves wherever possible by our racial heritage. Why is it that black has come to define whole nations, thus negating our African, Caribbean and Asian heritages? What nations are defined by the colour white?

Naming someone a black lesbian tells me nothing, it leaves me to assume that the person I'm about to meet could be of African, Asian-African, African-Caribbean, Asian-Caribbean, Asian, Latin American, Indigenous Australian descent and so forth. However, what is clear is that our first and only Black Lesbian and Gay Centre in Britain did try to provide for all the above groupings of people, since we were not provided for on the mainstream white lesbian and gay scene, which in turn has defined us as black, exotic and different.

However, the Centre has recently shifted towards an Afro-centric identity, by referring to lesbians and gay men of African-Caribbean descent only, or by acknowledging only the clubs and events which cater for this racial identity.

It seems that the 90s have seen a shift towards identifying around race rather than colour. Hence, socialising between African, Caribbean and Asian lesbians on the black scene is not so common as it was in the 80s. Perhaps, because there were so few of us about, we needed each other a lot more to cope with the racism on the scene. Whether or not we continue to provide more events around the definition of racial identity, rather than a colour identity black, what is important is that defining as black has been fundamental for many lesbians of African, Caribbean and Asian descent right up to the 90s.

THE SCENE: PART OF A BLACK LESBIAN IDENTITY

Part of being a black lesbian has meant socialising in our own separate spaces, where the culture of an event is specifically geared towards our music, food, and entertainment tastes. The mainstream lesbian scene in Britain has rarely catered for the needs of black lesbians. The scenario is that a black lesbian 'comes out' publicly about her sexuality, and feels an enormous desire to be among other lesbians. What she is not prepared for is the abandonment of her cultural tastes, and of reggae, bhangra, calypso, which she is likely to have grown up with. Similarly, she is not prepared for the absence of black women. Some black lesbians manage to assimilate into the mainstream, while others have created an underground scene for black lesbians to hang out in.

As a young woman in the 80s I was just desperate to rave. I discovered a new side of my black identity in blues and shabeams for black men and women, and anybody else who could cope with the vibe. Fresh to London, and in need of discovering my black self within the context of a black community, after growing up in a white middle class environment, this raving culture was fundamental. I learnt not to be 'English', a derogatory comment which was often thrown at me by black people in London.

Although I was a lesbian, women-only clubs frustrated me. They finished at 2 am if you were lucky, played awful disco music, and made you feel like a piece of rare exotica. Virginia Burke writes in the London Lesbian Line first information pack in the 1980s, "I became heartily sick of hearing stuff like, You coloureds can't half move, You're so lucky to have been born with the rhythm in your blood, Are you as good in bed as you are on the dance-floor?" [9]

Although comments like these in the inner cities were more familiar in the 80s, the racism on the scene is still present, and has affected the development of a black lesbian identity. During the 80s, as a group of black lesbians going out together, we were often denied access. We were told the club was for members only, or at full capacity. During the early 90s, lesbian and gay clubs were notorious for stopping black lesbians at the door, and vetting us about our sexuality. I've been turned away with friends and told it was members only; I then asked white women entering the club if they were members and they said no, but were allowed entry. I've picketed and boycotted clubs with many other black women because we had a similar story to tell.

Unfortunately, in the clubs that were more favourable towards black women, a part of myself I had just begun to discover was usually absent. There were few reflections of me, and the music didn't connect to part of my spirit and culture. But, ironically, when I discovered the black lesbian scene a part of myself was denied too. I was too wild, too outrageous.

What was great about the black lesbian clubs was to be in an environment of wall-to-wall women, rocking and swinging in uncompromising positions. A part of my black and lesbian identity was being nurtured. I could blend in, be invisible, be affirmed, and go home knowing there were plenty of other black women around me who loved women. They allowed black women to 'free up' and display the full richness of their sexual identities. Rather than dancing yourself to death on acid and techno all night, friends and lovers would intimately dance with each other all night long. Blues parties for black lesbians have existed in Britain since the 70s, and often in cities where there may have been no other group, or poetry events and performances for them. Frequented mainly by women of African-Caribbean descent, they are still an essential feature of our lesbian identities.

Such clubs have helped many black women come to terms with their lesbian self because they have provided a safe haven where black women can meet other black women, while positively affirming their culture and race identity.

ME RAVE

I raved last night
Until me legs them bite.
Lover woman pulls me to dance,
While me wife take a stance.

Me can't see right
Coz there is no light.
So me twist and wind
And enjoy the grind.

I turn to me wife
Who gives me strife.
The night soon done
So me hold my tongue.

The lights get bright
And me get a fright.
I turn to lover woman
Who a rock with my wife.

There has also been a strong scene for Asian lesbians and in fact their clubs have been more successful in the mainstream. Perhaps this is because clubs like Asia and Paradise, which existed in the 80s, catered for gay men and women of Asian descent. Shakti, an organisation for Asian lesbians and gay men, celebrated its tenth birthday in 1996. It is the longest running night club in London for Asian lesbians and gay men. Various types of Asian music, bhangra, new world and disco, are played, and it is attended by many other lesbians of African-

Caribbean and white European descent, along with a majority of Asian gays. There is also an underground scene of Asian lesbian parties which are promoted by word of mouth. I remember being at my first one, and having the privilege of seeing Asian women integrate their culture, race and sexual identity in harmony. It reminded me of how we as black lesbians are often forced into compromising our identities when we are socialising on the white lesbian and gay, and black heterosexual, scenes. With the latter our lesbianism is often absent, and with the former our culture is often absent. The first time I ever saw two black women being intimate with each other was in a black women's blues. I had only ever seen black women be intimate with white women in night-clubs, and I know this experience has been the same for many other black lesbians, and continues to be like this today.

In black women only spaces, African, Caribbean and Asian lesbians seem so much more alive, dynamic, and relaxed. It is hardly surprising that black women often go out in a group when on the mainstream. Yet journalist Megan Radclyffe writes while dissing the first anthology of black lesbian writings in Britain: "I'm fed up with black dykes who rage that the lesbian club scene is racist, but who stand in a posse and refuse to mix. If they don't like the atmosphere – and my advice is the same to anyone who objects to difference – go somewhere else." [10]

As black lesbians many of us have been forced to go somewhere else, rather than choose. Some of us have expended energy fighting for recognition, getting nowhere fast, while others have initiated events to welcome us.

The first national black lesbian conference, held in 1985, which brought together women of African and Asian descent, was a significant landmark in creating a strong and visible identity: "Zami I was and still is one of the greatest achievements of black lesbians. It paved the way for further conferences, gave confidence to those black lesbians who were frightened of coming out, and most of all it told the general public that we do exist, and in numbers." [11]

I can still remember the buzz when, at university, I was a day tripper to London. I remember one of my children's home sisters (who had been living in London for a few years) saying, 'I can't believe there are so many black lesbians, so many lesbians who look like me.'

"One of the highlights of life came in October 1985, when more than 200 black lesbians attended the first ever black lesbian conference at Tindlemanor, Featherstone Street. I would never have thought it possible to see so many black dykes under one roof, what a glorious day for an old fogey like me! (And as for the post conference social ... well ... !)", writes Virginia Burke.[12]

Perhaps it is inevitable that a black lesbian subculture has evolved, in order to maintain specific racial and cultural identities.

COMING OUT

DEAR MOTHER

Dear Mother

(The waves of the sea come crashing down)

I have something to tell you, but I don't know how.
Oh how I've loved you,
Appreciated you,
Believed in you.
Please don't judge me,
Please don't disown me,
I am still me

(Seagulls are screeching in the sky)

Dear Mother,

(The waves of the sea come tumbling down)

I am very happy here,
I wish you were here,
The sea,
The air,
The land is very beautiful,
And she is beautiful too.
Mother!

(The waves of the sea come cascading down)

I am not sick,
I am not evil,
I am not going through a phase,
Please don't blame yourself.
Dear Mother

(Seagulls are flying in the sky)

Oh dear,
I have something to tell you,
But I don't know how.
Mother!

(Thunder and lightening is in the sky)

Please listen,
I,
You,
We,
Have,
Found my African Princ...ess.

Dear Mother!

(Hailstone and rain is pouring from the sky)

There is this unspoken myth that lesbians of African, Caribbean and Asian descent are never out to their families. I know as many black lesbians out to their families as I do who are in the closet. It is true to say that there are many black families who are accepting of their daughters' sexuality. However, like the white communities, there are many who are in complete denial, disowning their daughters, and resorting to extreme homophobic measures like those put forward by some churches to try and 'save' their children from the devil.

Coming out can be two-fold for the black lesbian living in the West: once she is aware of her sexuality and discovers the lesbian scene, she is faced with the issues of being in the minority, and within a white Western culture, which can often be unfamiliar or hostile to her. We are faced with the choice of assimilating, staying at home, or being creative by setting up something which is affirming to our African, Caribbean or Asian cultures, values and attitudes.

I used to think that I had no 'coming out' issues. I had fallen in love aged 17 with a woman and wanted to tell the whole world. I had no black parents to confess to, and because I had grown up in institutions, and with white families, I was able to assimilate on the scene and feel a familiarity. Of course I regretted this, I thought I was missing out on a drama, I was envious of my black women friends who were happily out to their families.

However, as I write this book, I realise that coming out for me on the black lesbian scene was traumatic, and that I most definitely had a 'coming out' story to tell. I was labelled as weird, eccentric, and someone who dated the enemy. Because I was visible in my work as a journalist writing for *The Voice*, then the only black national newspaper in Britain, I assume there were certain expectations of me. Those which stated I should have an Afro-centric outlook on life, including what I wear, and that I would channel all my emotional, political, sexual and physical energy into the African and African-Caribbean community. I failed dismally; although politically most of my written words were acceptable, who I slept with, how I danced, and what I wore, were not.

In retrospect, even I have to admit that freelancing for the mainstream media including *The Guardian* and writing for *The Voice* during the day, while working at night as a go-go dancer, clad in top hat, tails and a strap-on dildo, at what was Europe's biggest women only club in London, Venus Rising, was perhaps a little incongruous.

I hasten to add that while many black women shook my hand on the night of my donning a strap-on, and confessed they had one (I hadn't the heart to say actually this was borrowed), they were more concerned about me and another black woman dancing behind bars, which they perceived to be a cage. For us, it was a great opportunity to dance the chaos, bouncing and swinging off the bars.

LUV UP WHITE GAL DEM

WHITE WOMAN

White woman
I have loved your chrysanthemum creamy skin
All blushed – freckled and tanned.
Turned on by flashes of black and white,
Juxtaposed in harmony
Between the giddy frenzy of our sheets.

The forces of two magnets.
Positive to negative,
Negative to positive.
Black flesh on white flesh
White flesh on black flesh,
Navel to navel,
Signalling unsolicited messages.

I've
Peaked,
Staccatoed,
Crescendoed.

I've loved your straight – wavy – kinky hair.
Golden – auburn – brown
Cascading around my breasts
Frolicking around my neck.

I've loved your sweet whispers – gentle caresses.
And as I delve deeper into your psyche,
Tongue on tongue,
Swishing – both pink
Vulva to vulva
I've let go of my inhibitions,
And have known this is true love.

You white woman.
I love you because
You are woman.
You are female.
You are lesbian.
You are a fundamental part of my identity.

Actions have consequences: in July 1996, a friend said to me, "I've always been aware of you, I remember someone pointing you out and stating, That's Valerie Mason-John, she's a journalist, writer, performer, outrageous, and only sleeps with white women." Although the last bit is a myth, it has been instrumental in shaping my identity. These comments fed into my insecurity, but more fundamentally, distanced me from some black women, and also made me an outsider. I was accused of selling out, letting the side down, and for being weird. In 1997 I told one of my African-Caribbean lesbian friends (who dates white women) that I had written a poem about loving white women, she said: "Publish and be damned."

SOLD OUT

Sold out
Bought out
Caught out

Bought out
Caught out
Sold out

Caught out
Sold out
Bought out

Hey sistren
Who's that you step with?
You call her a lover? A friend? A sister?

Turned White
Dropped the fight
Got no spite

Dropped the fight
Got no spite
Turned White

Got no spite
Turned White
Dropped the fight

Hey sistren
You never say you check pork
Them a legs like stork

Lost your mind
Can't you find
A black behind

Can't you find
A black behind
To grind

Lost your mind
Can't you find
A black behind

Hey sistren
What wrong with you?
Don't you like us too?

English girl
Traitor girl
Weird girl

Traitor girl
Weird girl
English girl

Weird girl
English girl
Traitor girl

Hey sistren
We think
Your politics stink

Sold out
Bought out
Caught out

Caught out
Bought out
Sold out

Bought out
Sold out
Caught out

Because there are fewer of us out and about on the scene, who we take for a lover is often noticed. Since the days of the first black lesbian group in London, the issue of black women having white lovers has rumbled like an earthquake.

"I stopped attending black lesbian group meetings because I went from being one of the corner-pins to being marginal. I was ostracised for leaving a black lover and having a relationship with a white woman. I was told I had let the side down and was accused of selling out." [13]

What is interesting is that the black gay male communities have established acceptable names to describe each other with, when referring to their sexual partners. In the Asian gay men's community, you are a Potato Queen if you go out only with white men, a Sticky Rice Queen if you're an Asian man who goes out only with Asian men, Chop Suey Queen if you go with anybody, and a white man who goes out only with Asian men is a Rice Queen.

In the African and African-Caribbean gay men's community, if they go out only with white men, they're a Snow Queen, and a white man who goes only with black men is a Dinge Queen. Sadly, I find Dinge Queen lacks the humour of the other terms, and is derogatory. Adding to this list, I cite that white women who go out only with black women are Dumpling dykes or roti dykes and black women who date only white women are Brussels Sprout dykes.

However, this terminology highlights how much of an issue mixed relationships are, and how they impact on our day to day lesbian or gay black identity. *Blast*, a publication by the Black Lesbian and Gay

Centre, reports: "White women with black men has been an eyesore for decades now. More recent trends indicate a hip attraction of white males to black females. But a more worrying and irreconcilable phenomenon is waiting in the wings. Will it ever take centre stage? Inter-racial gay and lesbian relationships. Sleeping with the enemy!! That's how it's perceived, isn't it?" [14]

The black national newspaper *The Voice* regularly runs articles on mixed relationships. In 1996, on the letters page, a heterosexual black woman wrote in and stated: "Forty per cent of black men date white females. This is a humiliating fact for us black women. Everywhere we turn black men are selling out, deliberately avoiding black women. What are we supposed to do, sit pretty and wait for black men to wake up? We are tired of being neglected so we are forced to look to other racial groups for partners." [15]

Though there are no statistics in the lesbian community for what percentage of black women regularly date white women and settle down together, it is most probably approximately twenty per cent, considering the number of black women out and visible on the scene. And who cares anyway?

As a black woman who has had intimate and sexual relationships with both black and white women, and will continue to do so, I have continually questioned myself and my politics. I have most definitely a strong sense of both my black self and lesbian self, and my personal choices have influenced my political concerns to be more global.

In Barbara Burford's short story 'The Threshing Floor', Elaine challenges Hannah over her love for a white woman. Left on her own she tentatively explores the issue: "And from there she had begun an examination for the first time of her love for this white woman. She had believed up till that moment, that love was something uncontrolled, outside even personal politics." [16]

Discovering 'The Threshing Floor' in 1987 was fundamental to my positive self image. It was so refreshing to read a positive, loving story between a black and a white woman. Not only was this story one of the first to explore inter-racial lesbian relationships, it was also unique in including a character (Hannah) who came from a children's home background. However, some may argue it was because of this fact that Hannah would be more likely to fall in love with a white woman. But it is a fact that black women from all different backgrounds and experiences have had successful and nourishing relationships with white women, while keeping a strong sense of their black identities.

Going out with white women has most definitely not made me any the less black, or diluted my politics. I accept I have three weaknesses: Belgian chocolates, champagne and women. I have the potential to love all women.

Loving white women was perhaps a little bit more acceptable in the 80s because there were fewer visible black lesbians on the scene. It's argued that since there are so many more visible black lesbians there is no need to have sexual or emotional relationships with white women. Inter-racial relationships with white women are perceived to be fraught with difficulties. Those of us who relate to white women are often accused of selling out on our culture, and of being out of touch with our black identities. This thinking "echoes the politics of the Black Power movement in the 1960s and 1970s, which advocated the adoption of complete blackness through lifestyle and appearance." [17]

However, part of a black lesbian identity has been caught up in the mainstream stereotype of us as black women, which does give justifiable reasons why many black women are suspicious of white women. While on a two-week course exploring anger with African and African-Caribbean women of all sexualities and ages ranging from 18 to 41, the common stereotypes which came up of black women were: aggressive, loud, criminals, sports people, entertainers, menial workers, and good in bed.

These stereotypes along with many others have filtered onto the lesbian scene. Often we are pushed into butch roles by white lesbians, and it's assumed that we are automatically 'good in bed'.

"Within the gay scene I have found that I am almost always expected to be the butch person in the partnership." [18]

"What really cracked me up though was the assumption that I would be a sex-machine in-between the sheets ... or that I would find white women irresistible. On occasion I would venture home with a woman, who would be near frothing at the mouth in anticipation of a wild night with the 'Black Stud'. Once in bed, however, I would proceed to make my political statement, by falling asleep or pretending to. This action would prompt cajolery, derision ... mainly insults. 'I thought you blacks were supposed to be passionate. Oi You! Wake Up!' " [19]

During the mid 80s, I was in a relationship with a white woman which had broken down. Unable to speak up and say, "No I don't want to be sexual anymore," I just lay there hoping she would be aware of my thoughts. After a month of me not responding to her amorous advances, she blurted out, "So it's not true what they say about black people in bed." Needless to say, this gave me the impetus to speak up and leave.

Similarly, the Asian lesbian community have the stereotypes of passive, submissive, demure. "For white people generally, being an Asian is something to do with curry, saris, brown skin, funny music, strange religions, something to do with ethnics." [20]

Such stereotypes placed on black women can only alienate us, and make us behave differently in white environments. Aggressive behaviour may well be triggered by the suspicion that a white woman is only speaking to a black woman because she wants to pick her up for sex. For some, to be in a sexual relationship with a white woman would be more alien than being in a relationship with a black man.

LUV UP BLACK GAL

BLACKWOMAN

Tall Black Woman
who walks so high
who walks so proud
Shake your dreads for me.

Tall Black Woman
who moves so regally
who moves so queenly
Whisper patois for me.

Tall Black Woman
who dresses so beautifully
who dresses so creatively
Throw a smile for me.

Tall Black Woman
who loves women
who loves her sexuality
Please look out for me.

Some black women have chosen to have sexual and intimate relationships only with black women. Long distance relationships between two black women have become more popular, since the black lesbian network between Britain and America, Britain and Canada, has been established through conferences and travelling.

Tired of meeting the same women at events, international networking has widened our population, and given us more access to potential black lovers.

STAR GAZING

Last night,
I sent you a star,
It bobbed along the roof tops,
Glided along the skyline,
And ferried along the sea.

From France it hitched a ride,
In Greece it hopped into a hot air balloon,
And floated up high in the sky,
Landing safely in New York,
All warm and cuddly for you.

So tonight,
Look out through your window,
Beyond your street block,
And you'll see your star,
Winking and waiting for you.

Connecting with black lesbians from other parts of the world has been an empowering experience. When a Chinese friend of mine came back from San Francisco she said she couldn't believe how many positive Asian lesbian reflections there were out on the scene. She wanted to get a plane straight back. I immediately understood her sentiments when I visited the city.

While out in San Francisco, I was so bowled over by meeting black lesbians who were old enough to be my mother, it affirmed a part of myself. In Britain there are few black lesbians over 50 who are publicly out, in fact it is those of us in our 30s who will set the example of an ageing black lesbian population in Britain.

Inevitably, a black lesbian separatist subculture has developed, out of those black women who have wanted to be supported totally by their own cultures. Black lesbian separatism for African, Caribbean and Asian women has been a fundamental source of personal growth, self-development, and common identity, without the hindrance of racism. It has allowed many black women to come to terms with their sexuality in a safe and nourishing environment, while also embracing their cultural and racial identities. During the 80s black lesbian separatism was for predominantly African, Caribbean and Asian women, and others from Latin America, who wanted to dialogue and socialise with each other. However, the 90s have seen a move towards different black racial identities, organising among themselves.

P.C. DEFINITIONS

Naming our sexual identity among black women has been an interesting, long, open debate. There is no general consensus on what we should or shouldn't call ourselves, though prefixing lesbian with black seems to be acceptable. Black lesbian denotes that our experiences are different from those of white lesbians.

I've always had difficulty speaking the word lesbian, because as a child it was associated with something which was negative, wrong and evil. And as an adult, it's the most familiar word which heterosexual people could throw at you in terms of abuse. Therefore lesbian has at times left a bad taste in my mouth.

Some black women dislike the term lesbian because of its Eurocentric connotations. Lesbian is essentially an Anglo-Saxon term, with its roots in Greek culture. It was the word used to describe the inhabitants of the Greek island, Lesbos, where the woman-loving poet Sappho lived during the sixth century BC. It's argued that lesbian refers only to a Eurocentric aesthetic, to a Western identity and lifestyle based on the emotional and sexual desire for, and relationships with, other women.

However, because of these facts, many black women are happy to define themselves as lesbian, because it is part of the European culture which they were brought up in, feel familiar with, and which supported them in their choice of sexuality.

I believe that the term lesbian is Western-centric, in the sense that to be an 'authentic' lesbian and live a lesbian lifestyle, you need the financial independence to exist without men and set up home on your own, or with other women.

In Asia and Africa, it is impossible for most women to leave their men and set up home with another woman, because so much in their cultures is structured towards their being heavily dependent on men for housing, money, food, and clothing.

In Western culture, as an African woman I have the ability to access a complete lesbian lifestyle, and therefore feel comfortable defining myself as a lesbian, within the context of this premise.

However I am a black lesbian, just as I am black British. The prefix is essential, because my oppression is multifaceted: racist, sexist and homophobic.

My favourite word is dyke, because it is so upfront and in your face. I was liberated when I came across the term during the early 80s. The term for me is reminiscent of a particular politic in the 80s, black and white lesbians organising together around the issues of anti-racism, imperialism, colonialism, indigenous global struggles and lesbian homophobia. 'Dyke' embraced parts of a lesbian separatist politic. Dykes went on lesbian strength marches, attended lesbian conferences and workshops, set up peace camps and occupations, socialised among women. Some black lesbians have preferred the term because it isn't attached to a place in Europe. Ironically, I have never felt the same compulsion to prefix it with black, perhaps because I associated it with lesbians who had active politics.

While researching the origins of dyke for '*Making Black Waves*', I was delighted when I discovered that its likely origin is in African-American culture. I was also delighted when I discovered that dyke derived from the American word 'bulldyke' and first appeared in Blues songs of the 1930s. For example, Bessie Jackson recorded 'B-D Blues' in 1935, which referred to bulldyke. Although in American slang dictionaries 'dyke' is associated with masculinity, for me it has been about the feminine, harnessing our strong and independent qualities, so much so that we are categorised as being stroppy, troublesome, aggressive and in yer face.

'Gay' I've only ever used when I've wanted to be out, but not frighten the living daylights out of naive heterosexuals. The term gay has always been more palatable. To state that you are a lesbian or dyke in the heterosexual world, you really have betrayed men. Gay has always meant to me 'women who have relationships with women', but within a heterosexual context: women who have never explored the political implications of being visibly out as a lesbian. Because of its association with men, originally derived from the French term *gai*, which was adopted in the British theatre to describe men who played female characters, it's not surprising that the term does not sit happily with most visibly out lesbians. When I think of gay, I see clones at Lesbian and Gay Pride and Mardi Gras events – white men, with gym designed bodies, in T-shirts, tight jeans and brandishing leather jackets.

'Queer' is one word which I've rarely heard black lesbians use in Britain. Perhaps it will become more popular with the new generation of black lesbians in their teens. I've associated queer with the most recent sexual revolution, in the sense that it has become increasingly acceptable to be out as a lesbian or gay man and still sleep with the opposite gender, and for heterosexuals to sleep with the same gender. The musical 'Voyeurz', starring the all woman band Fem to Fem, is an example of this. Lesbians, gay men, heterosexual and bisexual women and men displaying their sexuality in the same space, and exploring bondage and tantric sex games.

In the British lesbian and gay community queer has been popularised by mainly white organisations like ACT UP and Queer

Nation, which were inspired by the white North American experience. Therefore, it's not surprising that our community has not latched onto queer. However, there is a politic behind it, assimilating male and female homosexuality into the mainstream, through 'up front, in yer face' politics. As the label has become more popular within the mainstream lesbian community, I can only now perceive it as an opportunity for some lesbians to explore their heterosexuality and act out fantasies: for example, by going out 'packing' (stuffing a strap-on dildo down their knickers), picking up gay men in clubs to fuck. Hence, queer for me is about a new generation of people who can openly experiment with sex, without having to define or be classified into a sexuality grouping.

Because the names to define ourselves as women who have sex with women have mainly originated from a white Western experience, it has been important for some black lesbians to find other names which seem appropriate to their specific experience.

THE ZAMI IN ME

Zami is one of my anchors,
It heals me,
Soothes me,
Calms me.

It is at times,
The zami in me,
The zami in my friends,
The zami in my lovers.

Zami is one of my anchors,
It mirrors me,
Reflects me,
Shadows me.

It is at times,
The zami in me,
The zami in my friends,
The zami in my lovers.

Names which have been significant in defining a black lesbian identity in Britain have been Zami and Khush, the latter originating from a South Asian experience, the former from a Caribbean experience. The late Audre Lorde introduced Zami to our black lesbian culture in 1982, through her book '*Zami: A New Spelling of My Name*'. Zami originates from the island of Carriacou, and was used to describe women who had sexual and loving relationships with each other. Because it is specific to women, it was initially adopted by many black women from a wide range of racial backgrounds. This was reflected in the first two black lesbian conferences held in Britain, which were called Zami I and Zami II, respectively.

However, though Zami seemed a popular term of choice within the black lesbian blues and poetry scene, only a small part of the community actually used it. Hence, results of a questionnaire for '*Making Black Waves*' highlighted that few black lesbians knew what Zami meant, and even fewer defined themselves as this. Some respondents felt that because Zami is about a particular Caribbean experience, it didn't refer to them, and that it was not necessary to transfer the term to a black British experience. Thus, lesbian seemed more appropriate due to the reasons cited earlier.

Khush (pronounced 'hoosh'), was liberating for some Asian lesbians, because it gave them a term they could use from their Middle Eastern culture. It is an ancient Urdu word which means gay and happy, signifying liking and ecstatic pleasure. Khush was popularised in the South Asian lesbian and gay community by the British-based film director Pratibha Parmar, who called her television documentary 'Khush', which is about South Asian lesbians and gay men.

Similarly, black lesbians who aren't from this racial culture do not find the term appropriate, because the term does not come from their cultures or experience.

What has been empowering for black lesbians is to find other names and definitions which describe our sexuality in the languages of the different countries from which we originate. Some women have done this by reclaiming names from an African and African-Caribbean tradition, like mati, samtikm, waimi and lesbier. [21]

However, it seems that black lesbian and dyke are the reference points for many of us. Terms like Zami and Alice Walker's term Womanist seem more inclusive of those politically correct African-Caribbean lesbians or women who are woman identified or indeed happily bisexual.

The new labels of the 1990s like fag dyke (lesbians who identify with gay men's culture and identities) and drag kings (lesbians who dress up as men for fun) seem to be new identities emerging on the predominantly white lesbian scene.

However, it is inevitable that such identities will affect the African, Caribbean and Asian scene as we move into the millennium. North American culture is proof of that. Perhaps we'll adopt names from our own individual street cultures like ragga dyke, rude dyke, dance hall dyke, yardie dyke and any other dyke we fancy to be.

DYKE SPOTTING

SPOT THE DYKE

Is it the way she wears her
Caftan,
Saris,
African prints,
Dashikis,
Shalawar,
Or could it be her
Calvin Klein's,
501s,
Doc Martens?

Or is it the way she
Wraps her head,
Ties her hair,
Paints mehndi on her hands,
Swishes her dreads,
Or could it be,
The number one shave,

Natural hairstyle,
The baseball cap?

Or is it
'The Colour Purple' on her bookshelf,
'Feminist Fables' on her coffee table,
'Zami' in her bedroom,
Skin on her wall,
Or could it be
Kali on her shrine,
Nefertiti round her neck,
The piercing in her nose?

Or is it
The mountain bike she owns,
The Honda Suzuki she drives,
The job she does,
Or could it be
The axe in her ear,
The lager in her fridge?
Who cares?
If she's looking at me.

Spotting the black lesbian is an exciting game to play, because we are not as visible as the stereotypical white lesbian. Dressing down, burning bras and the cropped hair of the 1970s and 1980s was not the dress code for the majority. The way you look as a black woman has always been highly valued in black cultures. This ethos is similar to white working class culture; the poorer and more oppressed you are, the more emphasis is put on personal appearance.

Hair in both the African-Caribbean and Asian communities has also been a status symbol. Long beautiful well-kept hair has been important in our communities. Hence, black lesbians were chic long before the advent of lesbian chic in the early 1990s, which is always portrayed as a white phenomenon.

Therefore, the appearance of some black lesbians has not necessarily changed so dramatically from that of their black heterosexual sisters. What is different is that we are not dressing for men. What has distinguished us from our black heterosexual sister is the challenge many of us have taken on by stepping out of the status quo, by becoming women who love women, sexually, sensually, intimately, emotionally and spiritually.

As lesbians we have belonged to the wider mainstream stereo-typical lesbian community, and therefore our identities have been influenced by the radical women of the 70s and 80s who dared to abandon their conditioning.

The women's movement during this period, which included women of all sexualities, races, cultures and classes, provided the platform for the new female identity to evolve. Women dared to be public about their sexuality, women dared to leave violent husbands, women dared to challenge the concept of femininity and masculinity in women.

Many African, Caribbean and Asian women (like white women), found the courage to come out as lesbians. Some women did this by dressing down, and many African and African-Caribbean lesbians made this a public statement by loksing up their hair. In the early 80s we dared to grow dreds and walk down the high street with them uncovered.

I remember being stopped on the streets, in supermarkets, and being lectured by black men about why I should wrap my hair. Dreds were a symbol for many black lesbians in the 80s, and the majority of heterosexual women with dreds wore them under cover. The first black lesbian conference for African, Caribbean and Asian women Zami I in 1985 witnessed the boom of the natty dred dyke.

To wear dreds was and still is a political and spiritual statement. Up until the 80s, people who wore dreds were normally practising Rastafarians, and in this religion only men are allowed to show their hair in public. The Rasta was perceived how the Jamaican Yardie is perceived today: a gangster, drug dealer, and trouble maker. Both the black and white communities perceived the person with dreds as a drop-out, as dirty. While the black community was aggressive to the dred, the white community feared the dred, making anybody with dreds vulnerable on the streets.

Dorothea Smartt writes in an article published in *Everywoman* about her 'Medusa' poems: "Medusa was a name given to me by the kids next door when I started to loks up my hair in the 1980's."

Black women donning dreds in public was a powerful statement. She became more visible on the streets, more vulnerable to racism, and black men often kept their distance, often in awe and fear of her. Smartt names 'Medusa' after all the strong black women who have influenced her in the poem 'Medusa: Cuts Both Ways'.

However, by the late 1980s, the funky dred hairstyle was very popular among black women and black men. It was the beginning of making dredloks into a populist hairstyle for the mainstream black community. The style was characterised by shaving part of the head, while keeping some dreds on the head, and by bleaching and colouring them, making the hairstyle a trendy fashion.

Black lesbians began to shed their loks and change their hairstyle to the other extreme, a closely shaven head. Shaving your hair completely off was another step away from the Asian, African and Caribbean values and traditions. The bald head for dark-skinned black women challenged the whole myth of beauty in both the black and white communities. Hence, if you were dark you could at least have some beauty by having long beautiful hair. The times I was told by black men how brave I was for having a bald head. While many black lesbians played a significant role in popularising the bald head for black women in the early 90s, it has become acceptable in most circles for African-Caribbean women and their peers under 40 to have a shaved head.

While hairstyles have been significant in creating a black lesbian identity, clothing has also played a significant part in the 80s. Asian lesbians mixed Asian dress with male Western attire: wearing saris and dashikis with Doc Marten boots and leather jackets. This asiakeke fashion (blending traditional Asian cloth with Western fashions) was and still is very much a symbol of Asian lesbian identity. Similarly, although not so pronounced, is the afrekeke fashion in the African-Caribbean lesbian community, reclaiming traditional African prints and blending them with Western attire.

Symbols have also been part of the black lesbian community. The axe, perhaps the most popular, was worn by many black and white lesbians in the 80s. However, since the 90s, symbols have become passé, and the opinion among some women is that because the axe is supposed to originate from the Greek isle of Lesbos, it is a Eurocentric symbol.

However, I recently came across a dictionary of symbols and spontaneously looked up the axe. And to my surprise, I read the following, that the twin bladed axe described as complex is related to the sign Tau: "A symbol of the power of light...This double headed axe is to be found in a host of works of art from India to England, and specifically in the Mediterranean countries – in Africa and Crete." [22]

Though the axe today is associated with the labrys from Cretan culture, according to Luc Benoist the twin bladed axe is the same as the Hindu Vajra and Jove's Thunderbolt.

I used to think every woman who wore an axe in her ear was a lesbian, and that did cause a major embarrassment. While sitting next to a woman on a plane travelling to the same conference, I assumed she was a lesbian. After an interesting conversation about men and relationships, I asked, "What does your girlfriend do for a living?" She calmly corrected me by saying 'he'. Well she did have an axe in each ear and refer to her man as a 'partner'.

I must confess I used to think every black woman who had a push bike was a lesbian, but it nearly got me into trouble one day, so I changed my mind. I gave the cyclist a big dykey smile and she cussed. However, black women on cycles in Britain, especially in London, have become much more visible during the 90s, challenging the stereotype of the respectable conservative young black woman.

What is clear is that there is no one static identity of a black lesbian (or any lesbian). In fact, it seems to be harder to identify the black lesbian among the crowd. The stereotype belongs underground on the night life scene, in the blues and poetry gatherings. And the scene with its multifaceted identities only caters for the tiny minority who dare to go out and rave and be visible.

REFERENCES

1) Definition by the Black Lesbian and Gay Centre, London, 1985

2) Peter Fryer, *Staying Power*, Pluto Press, London, 1984

3) Savitri Hensman, 'A Retrospective Black Together Under One Banner', in V Mason-John (ed.), *Talking Black: African and Asian Lesbians Speak Out*, Cassell, London, 1995

4) V Mason-John and A Khambatta (eds), *Making Black Waves* (Lesbians Talk Series) Scarlet Press, original source interviewee, Aqueela Alam

5) Ibid., original source interviewee, Marlene Bogle

6) Savitri Hensman, op. cit.

7) V Mason-John and A Khambatta (eds), op. cit.

8) Ibid., original source

9) Virginia Burke, London Lesbian Line, information pack

10) Megan Radclyffe, *Time Out*, London, March 8, 1995

11) V Mason-John and A Khambatta (eds), op. cit.

12) Virginia Burke, op. cit.

13) V Mason-John and A Khambatta (eds), op. cit., original source interviewee, Femi Otitoju

14) Black Scene Talk BLAST, Black Lesbian and Gay Centre, London, August 1996

15) *The Voice*, page 8, July 30, 1996

16) Barbara Burford, *The Threshing Floor*, Firebrand, 1987

17) Savitri Hensman, op. cit.

18) Black Community of Zamis and Gay men/Bisexuals (BCOZAGBI), London, July 3, 1996

19) Virginia Burke, op. cit.

20) SHAKTI, Vol. 1. April/May 1989

21) A Zami Culture product by Zamimass London-Abena Onomaa

22) J E Cirlot, *Dictionary of Symbols*, Routledge Kegan Paul, 1963 (reprinted 1984)

SECTION THREE

SIN DYKES

A hard-hitting comedy which puts the sting in the story
of black and white relationships

Dedicated to the late Jenny White, writer, artist and journalist,
who believed in this play and encouraged me to stage it.
The spirit of you permeates *Sin Dykes*, thankyou.

The story of one woman's exploration of sexuality, as she comes face to
face with the issues of relationships between black and white, SM in
mixed relationships, and SM between black women. Set in the late
1990s, in London. Dykes are out of the closet. Black dykes openly do
SM, dykes openly sleep with gay men. There is dialogue, debate, and
outrage, but nobody is listening any more.

Sin Dykes was first presented in January 1998 at the Oval House
Theatre, London. The production was directed by Paul Everitt and
produced by Jennifer Dean; Flick Ansell was Stage Manager and
Lighting Designer; Tina Paulson was Sound Designer; Tamasin Rhymes
was Theatre Designer; Jo Fraser-Odin was Language Consultant; and
Jane Campbell was SM Consultant. The cast was as follows:

TRUDY	Suzann McLean
GILL	Kathryn Drake
KAT	Jo Fraser-Odin
BD	Gailen Manuel
CLIO	Queenie
TRACE	Paola Cavallin

The character of TRACE was renamed PIETRO for this production.

The play received no public funding and staging was made possible only
through sponsorship from the community, including: Sabine Baur,
Jennifer Dean, Jenny White, Diva magazine, QX magazine, Cyberdog
Paradiso, Prowler Soho, Sh!, FIST, Target Distribution and Oval House.

CHARACTERS

TRUDY:
> a Brixton babe, African-Caribbean, aged 25; non-specific black British accent; femme.

GILL:
> a scene dyke, white European, aged 32; non-specific English accent; butch/femme on the streets, butch between the sheets.

KAT:
> an afrekeke dyke, African-Caribbean, aged 33; Jamaican accent (patois); femme.

BD:
> a bull dyke lesbian, white English colonial, aged 40; English accent, with a trace of South African twang; bull dagger dyke, closet SM queen.

CLIO:
> a travelled black dyke, aged 28; Cockney ('Essex girl') accent; dominatrix, whether top or bottom, always in charge.

TRACE:
> an SM white dyke, who sleeps with gay men, and enjoys the role of the slave; as a slave she is submissive but butch and adores her mistress; when not in role of slave is laddish and cocky; when in slave role speaks only with her body.

PLACE: London: Diva's Bar; Trudy's bedroom; Gill's bedsit.

TIME: Late 1990s.

PRODUCTION NOTES

Set and props – The set for the first scene is a drinking bar, with a few tables and chairs. In the original production the bar was designed to be easily convertible into a double bed for use in the other scenes.

Stage action – Includes some physical theatre and mime, as indicated in the text.

Patois – Phrases used mainly in Kat's dialogue, often as oaths or terms of abuse, incude:
> 'bloodclart' or 'clart' = sanitary towel
> 'rasclart' = toilet paper
> 'ratied' (pron. to rhyme with 'parteyed') = backside
> 'under manners' = under her thumb

Clio's Cockney accent – Clio drops her h's throughout her dialogue, as in 'ave' for 'have' and 'be-ave' for 'behave'. This should sound natural, not 'stage' Cockney.

Dialogue – The / (back slash) signifies an overlap in dialogue. This indicates the point at which a following character's line should come in while the first character is still speaking.

Music – Popular club music accessible to both black and white women.

THE PLAY: SIN DYKES

Scene One

Diva's Bar. Night.

On stage there is a bar with tables and chairs (see Production Note).

The audience enter into a clubby atmosphere and are frisked by BD, *the owner of the bar.*

Music is playing. Disco lights flashing.

Other members of cast – CLIO, KAT, GILL, TRACE *and* TRUDY – *can be seen on stage dancing to the music.*

Once audience settle, stage lights slowly raise.

The tune 'Dance Hall Queen' (Bonza Mix) begins to play.

CLIO *begins to flirt with the dancers. She subtly goes up to each character in turn and dances with her. However, when she finally reaches* TRUDY, *the energy is different, their eyes meet, they connect, and move closer together, rhythmically.*

CLIO *and* TRUDY *dance in a sensual manner.* KAT, GILL *and* TRACE *are frozen in position, watching with jealousy.*

BD *makes her entrance from the auditorium, marching into her bar.* CLIO *and* TRUDY *continue dancing, to dimmed music.*

BD. Music off.

> *Music is turned down, but not completely off.* TRACE *turns to* KAT.

TRACE. Who's rattled her cage?

BD. It's like a bloody shabeam in here, lights on.

KAT. Oh come on, BD, you got to admit it's better than any peep show / you visit.

BD. Two minutes.

GILL. Can't you cope with the competition?

KAT. Give us a squeeze, what happened to a bit of / fun?

BD. Exactly. I'm the boss around here. Last orders.

TRACE. I'm leaving.

GILL. Is that a revelation? You've been leaving ever since you arrived.

TRACE. Well the scenery is nothing to die for.

GILL. If you don't like the furniture you know / what you can do.

BD. I said last orders.

> *Disco lights stop flashing and lights go to sudden black out.*

Scene Two

TRUDY's *bedroom. Morning after the club night.*
> *The loud sound of a radio alarm clock rings out.*
> *Lights come up on* TRUDY *and* CLIO, *they are entwined with each other.* CLIO's *hand appears and tugs at her shoulder.*

CLIO. Ere, where the ell do you think you're going?

TRUDY. Some of us do work / you know.

CLIO. Excuse me.

> TRUDY *snuggles back up to* CLIO.

TRUDY. What do you mean, 'Excuse me'?

CLIO. Oh great, you bring me ome for a shag, get stoned on your own dope / and pass out.

TRUDY. Alright, alright, you've made your point, I'm embarrassed enough as it is.

> *They cuddle, begin to kiss,* CLIO *pushes* TRUDY *affectionately away.*

CLIO. You're gorgeous you know, the way you looked at me in Diva's last night just sent me electric. I've been masturbating all night. Look, feel your / sheets.

TRUDY. Please! Stop! I can't be late for work again, BD will sack me.

CLIO. Fuck BD.

TRUDY. In her dreams.

> *They giggle and cuddle again, and hump a little, the radio alarm rings out again.*

TRUDY. I must get up for work. What time is it?

CLIO. It's sex time.

They playfully wrestle with each other.

CLIO. Ain't you into submission?

TRUDY. Right that's it. I'm getting up.

CLIO. Don't I turn you on? Or is it just my fantasy?

TRUDY. You know you do, I've been watching you for months.

CLIO. Ave you now?

TRUDY. Yeah, I remember the first time you walked into the bar, with your girlfriend.

CLIO. Girlfriend! More like ex.

TRUDY. Let me finish, huh, I remember thinking I've never seen two black women flaunt their sexuality so publicly. You were kissing and groping ...

CLIO. Give us a break sistah, she's an ex.

TRUDY. I know, but the point I'm making is that I've only ever seen two white women, or one black woman with a white woman, be so passionate in public.

CLIO. Where ave you been anging, oney?

TRUDY. I give up.

CLIO. No don't, you're turning me on.

TRUDY. Really! Do you feel the same way I do?

CLIO. That depends.

TRUDY. Last night I was so turned on. Your bum in those chaps looked so cute.

CLIO. Be-ave.

TRUDY. I am. (*Giggles.*)

CLIO. So you're not Ms Naive after all.

TRUDY. No, yes, no, what I'm trying to say is I've only seen white gals in chaps, and their buttocks are usually flat as pancakes.

CLIO *grabs her, they begin to play. All of a sudden* TRUDY *jumps out of bed looking terrified. She's dressed in baby doll nightwear.*

TRUDY. Shit, what the hell is that? (*Points.*)

CLIO. A labia piercing.

TRUDY. A what?

CLIO. A piercing.

TRUDY. Are you serious?

CLIO. No. Me cunt just appens to ave a Tampax dangling from it.

TRUDY. Right that's it, I'm taking a shower.

> TRUDY *exits leaving* CLIO *in bed.*

CLIO. What's the problem, don't you like diamantes?

TRUDY. No! I just like you.

CLIO. Like! Is that all? I thought you ad the ots for me all summer.

> *The sound of a shower begins. As* CLIO *speaks the shower gets louder and louder.* CLIO's *speech is also very physical and humorous, she produces some of the things she speaks about and plays with them.*

CLIO. Hey Trudy, I don't scratch or bite, you know. God knows what you'll tell the gals at work tonight. Just to fill you in. I fist, I pack, and whip, safe sex of course. Dental dams, gloves, and condoms. If you come back to bed, I'll and cuff yer to the bed posts. Tie you up and make love to you. All with your consent, your permission and your undying love of course. Sold out of course, I know that's what your thinking. Black girls are vanilla dykes. Well this one is made of Äagen Dazs, mate, chocolate chick cookie to be precise. Oh well, better wear a dog collar next time I go cruising, obviously ankies in back pockets are too confusing for Brixton babes.

> *Sound of shower abruptly stops.*

TRUDY (*shouts from back stage*). Right, that's it, out now, I'm off to work.

CLIO. Oh come on babe, where's your sense of umour?

TRUDY. I hate to remind you, but I consented to sleep only. Put your clothes on and leave.

CLIO. It ain't appening, is it?

> *Black out.*

Scene Three

Diva's Bar. Sunday evening.
Lights up. BD *and* TRUDY *in mid-confrontation,* GILL *and* KAT *in the background*

BD. Late again.

TRUDY. Give us a break, it's only 8.15 –

BD. It isn't fair Trudy, you're always late, and with no suitable excuse. Cleaning up the mess from the night before / is all part of the job.

TRUDY. All-right, all-right, all-right.

BD. One last chance Trudy, and then you're out. There are plenty more cute girlies who can pull a pint just as good as you, and don't mind breaking a nail or two.

> BD *exits and* TRUDY *walks up to the bar, where* GILL *and* KAT *have been avidly watching the confrontation.* GILL *and* KAT *giggle.*

KAT. So what did Madam BD have to say?

TRUDY. Oh the usual.

KAT. Shush, she's in her office.

GILL. Oh come on, I'm more interested in your bit of homework last night.

KAT. Give the girl a squeeze, she hasn't even taken her coat off. She'll tell us all in good time, Gill.

GILL. I'm not jealous.

KAT. Who mentioned jealous? I wasn't thinking of any such thing. Surely you're over the break-up by now.

GILL. Is jealousy supposed to be one of those emotions I should pretend not to have?

KAT. You know what I mean.

GILL. No I don't.

TRUDY. Hey, do I get to say anything, before you two kill each other?

> GILL *and* KAT *turn to* TRUDY *and speak together:*

GILL. So come on spill the beans.

KAT. So come on spill the beans.

TRUDY. I fell asleep.

KAT. Bitch, some 1990s' dyke.

GILL. Didn't I teach you anything?

TRUDY. I couldn't cope with all her piercings.

KAT. You need educating, African sistahs loveup their jewellery.

GILL. Not that type / of jewellery.

TRUDY. Shush, BD's on the warpath, speak to you later. (*Scowls at* GILL.)

> BD *enters.*

BD. What do you call this? A WI meeting.

TRUDY. Actually it's a witch's circle.

BD. Button it Trudy, you're already in trouble. I want some action in here tonight. You all looked like you had just risen from the morgue yesterday. Smiles, polite manner, and no flirting. Gill, you're glass collecting / this shift. And I want breakages down, at the rate it's going, they'll be more staff than glasses.

GILL. Again!

KAT. That's out of order, we've been stuck behind the bar all week, BD.

BD. You heard me, now think yourself lucky, with all those nymphs you've been able to entertain.

KAT (*sucks teeth*). This place is full of funeral and diesel dykes.

BD. Exactly. Just your type, I would have thought, Kat.

> KAT, GILL *and* TRUDY *look off stage and laugh.*

KAT. Are you for real? Sorry BD, I'm married.

TRUDY. Married, since when?

BD. Get to work. If it's quiet you can swap around but I want everything to run like clockwork tonight. Well, what are you all staring at? Get this place sparkling, before the punters arrive. And Trudy, I'll see you back here after hours.

> BD *exits. The others giggle, and mimic* BD*'s bull daggerish swagger.*

GILL. You better watch out, I think she's leaking after you.

TRUDY. Well that makes two of you, doesn't it?

GILL. OK, smart arse, one day you'll fall flat on your face, and then we'll see who's smiling.

KAT. You two, keep your domestics at home.

GILL. You're a fine one to talk.

TRUDY. Yeah, since when have you and Alfia been married?

KAT. Later.

> TRUDY, GILL *and* KAT *begin to do some work: polishing glasses, wiping down bar, etc. They look off stage and begin commenting on the punters.*

GILL. Check those fingernails out.

TRUDY. Where?

KAT. Fancy having those inside you.

> GILL *laughs, spreads her hand out and chases* KAT *and* TRUDY, *both screaming.*

GILL. Freddy Krueger, here I come.

> *They all crack up laughing, and begin to get the bar ready.*

TRUDY. Who's that?

KAT. Me nah no.

TRUDY. She's a bit of alright.

KAT. Hands off, it's my turn to wind and grind tonight, daughter (*pronounced 'darter'*).

TRUDY. I thought you weren't into white gal dem?

GILL. She's pre-menstrual.

> KAT *sucks her teeth, and takes a look off stage.*

KAT. She ah definitely fit.

TRUDY. Fancy taking her home for the night?

GILL. You can use my bedsit if you like.

KAT. Girl, you too damn fresh, and talking of taking punters home, when are you going to give us the gory details?

Another punter TRACE *enters. Mutual hostility and eyeballing between her and* GILL.

TRACE. Half a pint of lager?

KAT. Hi Trace, how's it going?

TRACE. Young free and single.

KAT. Cruising tonight?

TRACE. Am I that obvious?

GILL. Yes.

TRACE ignores GILL *and turns to* KAT. GILL *walks off and collects some glasses.*

TRACE. What's the clientele like?

KAT. Gaby and her posse are here.

TRACE. No thanks, I'll keep well away from that crowd.

KAT. Can't you take the pressure?

TRACE. You know the score.

KAT. Take a wander, you never know what you might find. Can't talk now, catch you later.

TRACE. Yeah and tell Gill to get off my case. (*Walks off.*)

GILL brings some glasses up to the bar.

GILL. Kat, your date for the night is the cutest ever feline faggot.

KAT. Are you for real?

TRUDY. You're joking.

GILL. Take a look, they say the best looking dykes are gay boys. Larry would like a Beck's.

KAT and TRUDY *look off stage,* KAT *reaches for the Beck's and slams the bottle on the bar.*

GILL. I take it you won't be needing my keys.

KAT. I've always preferred my own.

GILL. Oh sorry darling, two pints.

> TRUDY *pours the pints and* GILL *leaves with the tray.*

TRUDY. Look who's just walked through the door.

KAT. Who?

TRUDY. Billy and Claire, they've just gone into the pool room. Didn't take them long to make up after last week's drama.

KAT. Me nah boddah with those two you know. Me have no time for people who wash their dirty linen in public.

TRUDY. You can be so hard sometimes.

> GILL *walks back up to the bar.*

GILL. It's quiet now, I've come for the second instalment.

KAT. Yes man, me forget to ratied.

TRUDY. Well no thanks to you.

GILL. I don't believe it, what have I got to do with your one night stand?

TRUDY. I got stoned on that grass I scored off you last night. It knocked me out before the count of 10.

KAT. You better watch out she doesn't lace your drink, next time you pull a woman.

GILL. Ha ha, you're so funny. Come on, Trudy, is that the reason? The grass isn't that strong.

TRUDY. Well / she wouldn't let / me out of the bed every time I went to get up she enticed me back.

GILL. I knew it (*at first /*).

GILL. Listen (*at second /*).

KAT. Eh eh is that it? Nah boddah tell me you just jump braps in and out of bed siddam so, and nuttin a go-on.

TRUDY. That's it.

GILL. What about the piercings?

GILL. Me warn you, the woman weird, with her bottom hanging out of those leather trousers.

TRUDY. You call yourselves friends?

> BD *enters and beckons towards the bar.*

BD. Gill!

GILL. I better go, looks like there's trouble at the door.

> GILL *exits with* BD.

KAT. Me di think say tonight would a quiet, but me corn toe already a burn me.

TRUDY. Sunday normally is.

KAT. I want to be home early.

TRUDY. That reminds me – Since you're married, how is the Mrs?

KAT. Fine, things sweet right now. Not much sex though. We're in that phase of eating tea together while watching Brookie, going to the market on Saturdays, and visiting the rellies on Sunday.

TRUDY. It sounds a wee bit patriarchal.

KAT. That's marriage, but it's good for me.

TRUDY. Yeah I reckon.

KAT. I know you're surprised, but I'm enjoying just relaxing, and getting into my college work. It's good for me. Keeps me out of trouble.

TRUDY. Sounds like you're ageing rapidly.

KAT. No, just enjoying being under manners, she's got me well sussed. It happens to the best of us. And you no say every dog have him day, and dis is mine.

TRUDY. Speak for yourself, Kat. Anyway how are you coping, for money?

KAT. Don't ask. As you know, a month after beginning my social work course Alfia was made redundant. It's been a nightmare.

TRUDY. What about the mortgage?

KAT. I'm grafting, a bit of this and that, you know how it goes so.

TRUDY. Shush, BD's on the prowl again, we better stop talking.

KAT. We should be stock taking.

> TRUDY *and* KAT *begin to check the stock.* TRUDY *exits behind bar, and re-enters with a crate of beer. She puts it on the bar and looks off stage, catching sight of something. She stops and watches intently, and suddenly turns to* KAT.

TRUDY. Hey, is that your friend Trace?

KAT. Where?

TRUDY. Look over there. She's smooching with that woman, I mean that guy you fancied earlier.

KAT (*sucks teeth*). Joke's over. Didn't take Trace long.

TRUDY. What do you mean? I thought she was a dyke.

KAT. She is. She's most probably packing for the night.

TRUDY. Packing?

KAT. Of course, that's why you and Gill split / up.

TRUDY. That's not true. We split up ... Why the hell should I defend myself? ... Is 'packing' something else I'm missing out on?

KAT. You're such a babe, when I really take you under my wing and show you one or two tings, you'll never look at a white girl again.

TRUDY. Kat.

KAT. Trudy, you got no excuse to check white gal, now you know where the black women's scene is.

TRUDY. Look, Gill might have her faults, but so have you and I. I'll go out with who I fancy.

KAT. One thing you've got to understand about some of these 1990s white girls is that they say it's alright to screw a man and call yourself a dyke. It's the phase at the moment, packing a dildo down their Calvin Klein's, and picking up cute looking gay men. It's all the rage. They call it queer.

TRUDY. You're so informed, have you tried it?

KAT. I'm a one-woman-only, me dear.

TRUDY. Since when has that stopped you?

KAT. Girl, you're feisty bad you know. (*Sucks teeth.*)

TRUDY. Anything else I need to know?

KAT. Why don't you join your white friends dem, and book up on one of those genderbending courses. They'll teach you to strap your breasts down, don a tash, and how to bulge in the right places.

TRUDY. Oh you're so funny, you make me cringe.

> KAT *picks up duster from the bar rolls it up and hands it to* TRUDY.

KAT. Here, stuff these down your pants.

TRUDY. Too big for my knickers, sistren.

> *They crack up laughing, but are interrupted by* BD *who enters looking flustered. She pours herself a drink at the bar.* CLIO *appears on a dog collar, with* TRACE *holding the lead. She stands at the doorway and stares at* TRUDY. TRACE *leads* CLIO *who walks proudly and gracefully, clicking her metal tipped heals on the floor. They freeze.*

KAT. But stop, what the ras a go-on?

BD. None of your ethnic talk, girls. You might alienate the customers.

> KAT *sucks her teeth and throws a look at* TRUDY.

KAT. You know that's definitely out of order, BD.

BD. Sorry darlings, just a little joke.

KAT. Any more jokes like that, you can flush down the loo with the rest of your shit.

BD. Sorry, sweetie pie. I'll make it up to you later.

KAT. No thanks, keep it.

> BD *takes her drink and sits at a table. Lights go up on* CLIO *and her white slave* TRACE.

KAT. Trudy to rasclart, is that una gal wey (*the girl who*) you pick up last night?

TRUDY. You know it is.

KAT. But wait, but what she a tink she a do?

TRUDY. Why don't you ask her?

KAT. Me talk to dat? Forget it. Tell me something. So what you do last night? You never no say she into bondage. No wonder you never wan talk bout it.

TRUDY. You never know who you may end up in bed with. You nearly ended up in bed with a man / tonight.

KAT. This is serious gal. She's into / SM.

TRUDY. You're such a hypocrite, Kat. Gill's a self-defined SM dyke. You smoke her dope, smile, and rub up against her.

KAT. But this different.

> GILL *enters and takes* CLIO *to a table.* CLIO *continues to stand.* BD *catches her attention. They smile.* BD *pulls a black-and-white hanky from her bra and blows her nose.* GILL *notices while bringing some glasses up to the bar.*

GILL. Guess what girls? I told you BD's into black tops.

TRUDY. Not now Gill later.

GILL. What's going on? Black girls only, is it?

TRUDY. Gill, is that necessary?

GILL. It's been tense out there.

TRUDY. It's tense in here too.

> GILL *leaves bar and continues to collect bottles.*

KAT. So what your saying, Trudy?

TRUDY. Look, I told you what happened last night.

KAT. Me no say you have to start dating black women but you can forget that one she's a coconut. Sistahs like her are tearing our black community apart.

TRUDY. If you've got a problem, tell her.

> GILL *brings* CLIO *to the bar with the white woman still holding the leash.* GILL *tries to act cool as if everything is normal.* CLIO *notices* KAT's *reaction to her. Playfully she tries to interact,* KAT *sucks her teeth.*

CLIO. Alright, sweet art?

KAT. Me nah serve.

CLIO. I'll come dressed all Afrekeke for you, next time, dready.

KAT. Black women like you are renk.

CLIO. They crucified your Lord on the cross, natty.

KAT. You too damn fresh.

CLIO. Pulpit's crumbling, darling.

> KAT *sucks her teeth, steps back and observes.* CLIO *turns to* TRUDY, *smiles and becomes seductive.*

CLIO. Hi babe, meet me slave. She's brought me along as a gift for you.

TRUDY. 'Not tonight Josephine,' what did you say you were drinking?

CLIO. I didn't. Don't you play?

TRUDY. I work too hard. Remember? Now, what would you like to drink?

CLIO. Um ... I'll ave a 'Sloe Comfortable Screw', an 'In Between the Sheets' for you, and a 'Bloody Mary' for me slave.

TRUDY. Sorry, we don't do cocktails. Lager, spirits or wine.

CLIO. I prefer clittails myself, ow about you?

TRUDY. Chocolate fudge with a crunch.

CLIO. Impressive! Oh well, it will ave to be just two glasses of water, and anything your crunch desires.

TRUDY. That will be two pounds exactly. Thank you.

CLIO. Ave you got time for a break?

KAT. Yeah, Trudy has got all the time it takes for you to remove that dog collar. Are you off your box or what?

TRUDY. Kat, leave it out. Give me five minutes.

CLIO. My girl doesn't seem to like my dress sense.

TRUDY. No, and neither do I, and Kat is a friend.

> GILL *comes up to the bar and joins* KAT.

GILL. Can I be of any help?

TRUDY. Yes, distract Kat.

> CLIO *and* TRUDY *sit at a table.* GILL *and* KAT *finish off the stock check.* CLIO *notices* GILL.

CLIO. Who's that?

TRUDY. I thought you wanted to speak to me.

CLIO. I do, I came to say sorry.

TRUDY. I can see you took great lengths to apologise.

CLIO. You can whip me for being a bad girl if you want.

TRUDY. It's not my style.

CLIO. Ow about a play date?

TRUDY. What's a play date?

CLIO. Oh you know, dressing up, strawberries and cream.

> BD *gets up from her table.*

TRUDY. I've got to get back to work. She's the boss.

CLIO. Ere, take my card. Give me a call next week. Take a night off work for a change.

> BD *saunters up to the table where* TRUDY *is sitting.*

BD. Excuse me please, you seem to be upsetting the clientele. This is a vanilla club, no chains allowed.

TRUDY. That's not true. And the bar is empty.

BD. Exactly. I'm the boss, no leather.

> BD *continues to assert her power,* TRUDY *walks back to the bar.* CLIO *stands, beckons to* TRACE *who pulls a black hanky from* CLIO's *left back pocket, and presents it to* CLIO. *She whips* BD *with it.*

CLIO. Like a bit of bondage, do we?

> CLIO *beckons* TRACE *again and she pulls a grey hanky from her back left pocket and presents it to* CLIO. *She slaps* BD *around the face.* BD *smiles.*

CLIO. Or would you prefer some eavy SM whipping?

BD. When are you visiting my Trudy again?

CLIO. That depends when you give er the night off from this dump.

BD. That could be arranged.

> CLIO *laughs, beckons to* TRACE *who pulls an orange hanky from her right pocket, and polishes* CLIO's *boots.* TRACE *gets carried away and raises her backside for a slap.* CLIO *slaps her and beckons* TRACE *for the hanky,* CLIO *turns her back on* BD, *and throws the hanky over her shoulder.*

CLIO. Not tonight, I'm just looking.

> TRACE *picks the black and grey hankies from the floor, and they exit,* TRACE *leading* CLIO *off.* GILL *rings the bell.*

GILL. Last orders.

> BD *goes to her office while the others clean up for the night.*

KAT. Trudy, will you cover for me? I'm going to be late next shift.

GILL. You're not going awol, are you?

KAT (*sucks her teeth*). Trudy, do you mind swapping?

TRUDY. As long as you don't mind scrubbing the cellars tonight, I'll just finish of drying these glasses.

GILL. BD gave you that for being late.

TRUDY. Yep, but looks like Kat's volunteering.

GILL. Right I'm off. (KAT *and* TRUDY *ignore her.*) What's up with you two?

TRUDY. Don't worry, we'll get over it. I'll ring you when I get home.

> GILL *exits.*

KAT. Me never get over how you love up white and weird women so.

> TRUDY *stops drying the glasses and flings the tea towel down.*

TRUDY. What's wrong with white women?

KAT. What's wrong with black women?

TRUDY. Nothing.

KAT. So why you never boddah date them?

TRUDY. Why do you have to keep on giving me a hard time about who I sleep with?

KAT. It's not so much who you fuck, it's who you choose to have relationships with.

TRUDY. Why?

> KAT *sits on bar facing the audience,* TRUDY *leans on the bar facing the audience.*

KAT. Because I can't understand how you can have relationships with the enemy. Know your history, girl, white people have persecuted so many of our people. How can you hang with someone who reminds you of slavery?

TRUDY. That was centuries ago.

KAT. It's still happening now, look around you. I've got four brothers and all of them have done time. Three behind bars, and the fourth is in a psychiatric unit.

TRUDY. They must have done something.

> TRUDY *finishes polishing the glasses.*

KAT. Something, yes me dear, Alvin tried to protect his friend from being beaten by the police, Hugh got fed up of being told 'Sorry, the job is gone' when he arrived for interview, and lashed out. When Bradley left school, he realised him and thousands of other black men weren't going to be Pele, so he became pimp and drug dealer, and the youngest cracked up on his eighteenth birthday, and was sectioned. So yes, me dear, oona right, them a do something, them a react against this racist system.

TRUDY. But not all white people are racist?

KAT. Of course they are, this society breeds them. Them can't help it, oona call it white privilege.

TRUDY. You're friends with Gill.

KAT. That different. Me nah boddah with pork. I don't want to wake up every morning to a face which reminds me of those kids at school, who asked, 'Wogga matter? Are you all white? Ah nigger mind, go black home, eat your coon flakes and you'll be all white in the morning'.

> TRUDY *laughs and* KAT *scowls.*

TRUDY. Oh come on Kat, you've got to laugh, it's so awful it seems unreal. I suppose you've got a point, but it's not my experience, and I don't go out with women like that. So tell me, who should I go out with, since Clio doesn't fit the bill?

KAT. If them have something to give you, take it but don't stay. Find yourself a nice Nubian queen. Them plenty out there, so fine and sweet.

TRUDY. I love women, and I refuse to be trapped by my colour. I won't compromise myself for anybody. Take me or leave me.

KAT. You better leave, me have business to attend to. Nah boddah tink say me finish with you yet, we still have tings to talk bout.

TRUDY. Just remember to give my apologies to BD.

> TRUDY *puts out her hand to touch* KAT, KAT *slaps it.*

KAT. Later.

> KAT *sucks her teeth,* TRUDY *exits switching the lights off.*
> KAT *hides behind bar in black out and pretends to be* TRUDY.
> BD *enters bar, switches a dim light on, and walks to the bar. She runs her finger along the bar checking for dust and sensually picks up a glass on the bar.*

BD. Glasses, glasses on the bar, who's the sexiest one by far?

KAT. Madame BD is of course.

BD. Is that you, Trudy? Oh my honeysuckle, you've finally decided to play with me. What kept you my petal? No need to scrub floors anymore, come and sit behind the bar. (*Lights become brighter.*) No, don't come any closer, I'll tell you the rules. You'll be safe in my hands, it's a simple routine. (*Lights fade and a spot appears on a table.* BD *walks to the table and sits with legs straddled. As she speaks she takes her trousers and jeans off, revealing sexy suspenders – done in sync with the dialogue.*) I can't believe my Trudy has finally come to me. (*Excited gasp.*) It's like Christmas. I bought you some suspenders today so you could wear them for me. I wanted to surprise you. Have you found them? They're wrapped in white lace, with nipple clamps and knickers to match. Oh silly me, they're in the cupboard, in one of the old ice buckets. This afternoon I imagined you wearing the knickers over the suspenders so I could pull them down, leaving your stockinged ebony legs straddled apart. I placed my head between your feet, and you bent over, gently squeezing my breasts, and I waited for you to drip all over my face. Are you ready for me? Have you fastened the collar to your neck. How silly of me! I nearly forgot, shall I help you?

KAT (*in* TRUDY'*s voice*). No, I'm OK.

BD. That's good, because I don't want to spoil our fun. Ooooh I've waited so long for you. Just one more thing and then we'll both be ready to play. In the drawer are my favourite toys, handcuffs and a whip for you. You get to whip me if you handcuff one of your arms to the cupboard. Will you play, Trudy? No, don't answer, just throw the keys back. (KAT *throws the keys onto the bar floor from behind the bar*.) Now there's a good girl. Are you dressed for me? I can't hear you, sweetie pie, I know you're out there. (BD *gets up from her chair and puts her black lacey cloak on. She begins to walk towards the bar.*) I'm coming Trudy, oooh I'm coming, I can't hear your whip Trudy, crack the whip. (BD *reaches the bar and peers over. She recoils.*) Kat!

> *Lights come up on bar with* 'Kat!'. KAT *remains hidden from the audience.*

KAT. What's the matter, I thought all blacks look the same?

BD. Kat! It's not Tuesday. Where's my Trudy?

KAT. We swapped shifts, she sends her apologies.

BD. Where's my Trudy?

KAT. Trudy's never going to come, I need the extra cash, and you've had some fun, what more can a woman ask for?

BD. You're still dressed! You've only locked yourself to the cupboard. You've spoilt my game, it will never be the same. Broken the rules, naughty girls don't get paid.

KAT. Cha give me my money.

BD. Money, what money? You haven't earnt it.

KAT. Give me my bloodclart money.

> KAT *throws the underwear at* BD's *feet, with her free hand.* BD *picks them up and sniffs them.*

BD. Trudy's underwear, poor little things.

KAT. Me want me money.

>BD *walks towards her chair catches sight of the key. Picks up key and smiles.*

BD. Money or key, Kat? Naughty girls get punished.

>KAT *takes hold of the handcuff and tries to pull it off.*

KAT. Give me my money.

>BD *throws a roll of notes on the floor, and walks back into the office, slamming the door.* KAT *tries pulling at the handcuffs again but nothing happens. She curses out aloud. She pulls at the dangling handcuff again.*
>*The lights slowly fade to a blackout.*
>*The sound of a handcuff falling to the floor immediately follows the blackout.*

KAT. Lord have mercy.

>TRACE *and* CLIO *enter.* TRACE *is dressed in her laddish clothing. She switches the light on.*

CLIO. Smells of sex in ere, look, over ere, some one's lost an andcuff.

TRACE. Looks like you're late, mate, BD's already been served by one of her staff. If we wait she may come up for seconds, depends on her mood.

CLIO. So what are my chances of providing a service for BD and getting Trudy the night off?

TRACE. BD no problem, as for Trudy, she's a strange fish.

CLIO. What do you reckon, Trace?

TRACE. Not sure, Clio, I know she's still into Gill even though they don't do sex.

CLIO. I want er.

TRACE. What's got into my mistress? She's just a babe.

CLIO. I've been wet day and night since I met er, they call it chemistry, mate.

TRACE. My guess is you frightened the hell out of her earlier.

CLIO. You're my slave, it was your job to seduce er.

TRACE. Mine, why me?

CLIO. I ad Kat to deal with, the wretch kept on trying to distract my attention. Look, I need you to find out if she fancies me. I'm going crazy inside.

TRACE. Is it just a fuck you want, coz I know for a fact Trudy definitely isn't a one night stand girl. She's far too respectable / for that.

CLIO. Shut the trap up.

TRACE. She's the marrying kind.

CLIO. Great, that explains it.

TRACE. What?

CLIO. Nobody ever goes to bed with Clio without doing sex.

> TRACE *laughs and pats* CLIO *on her back.*

TRACE. Oh, so she's one of those virginal girls, opens up your heart, fucks you in the head, gets you addicted, and hooks you into her neurotic drama of 'Not tonight, I don't know you well enough'. Next, I'll be taking my mistress to therapy.

CLIO. Sounds like you've got a broken art.

TRACE. No, just a hole in the head from babes like Trudy.

CLIO. So I like the girl, she's kinda special, fresh, not contaminated by all that feminist and Afrocentric crap.

TRACE. Looks like BD's in recovery, you're out of luck Clio.

CLIO. Trace, sort it!

> *They exit turning the lights out.*

Scene Four

GILL's *bedsit. The next day.*

GILL *is in bed nestled under the duvet. Telephone by bedside dresser rings. She stirs. It rings again. An arm appears from beneath duvet and grabs receiver, pulling it under the covers.*

GILL (*speaking from under duvet*). Hello ... (*Slams receiver down. Sound of another phone ringing, similar bell. Sits up in bed, looks around room, and suddenly grabs jacket from a chair beside bed. Pulls a mobile out.*) Of course you've bloody woken me up ... What time is it? ... You're joking, ring me later.

> *Snaps mobile shut and switches it off, puts it back on chair, and snuggles under duvet. Sound of first phone again, she ignores it. Goes to grab the mobile, and stops midway, realising it's telephone set. Picks up receiver and lies back down. Pauses in following should be long enough to allow* GILL *to be seen reacting variously to the other person.*

GILL. Wrong number, ring 999 ... I don't care how urgent it is ... No you can't come round ... I'm not a bloody locksmith ... What type of key ... Handcuffs! (*Sits up in bed.*) What, like the pigs use? ... Am I supposed to laugh? ... Actually I gave them back with the uniform, sorry ... No! ... That's your problem, I'm wrecked, I need my sleep ... I'll look, but that's all I'm doing. Hold on.

> *Puts receiver down and bends over bed, pulls a small trunk from beneath bed. Opens it and rummages around. Closes the trunk and pushes it back under bed, and picks receiver up.*

GILL. You're in luck ... No promises it will fit ... Don't push your luck ... No! ... Tomorrow ... Five hours ... Three ... One and a half, I need to chill.

> *Hangs up, leaving the phone off the hook. Aggressively throws herself under duvet. Door bell rings.*

GILL (*shouts from beneath her duvet*). I'm out.

> TRUDY *lets herself in. She carries a bag.* GILL *pulls the duvet off her face.*

TRUDY. Are you alright?

GILL. Oh just a bad dream.

> TRUDY *moves the clothes and phone off the chair and sits down.*
> *She looks around the room.*

TRUDY. You're not going to stay in bed all day?

GILL. Oh not now, I'm sleeping.

TRUDY. No peace for the wicked.

GILL. Look, entertain yourself.

TRUDY. How comes you're in bed alone?

GILL (*sits up in bed*). Oh you know how it is. I was up the Rub Club last night, dropped an E, and spent half the night fisting in the toilets. I ran out of KY and rubber gloves. And then Suzanne came along and propositioned me.

TRUDY. Sometimes you're so boring. Obviously the E still hasn't worn off. Why don't you admit you're losing your charm?

GILL. Now I might be on E, but I'm not stupid. You didn't come all the way over here, to give me a hard time. You normally ring me to do that. And if you did, you know where the front door is.

TRUDY. I've brought you breakfast.

GILL. What's the celebration?

TRUDY. Six months of separation.

GILL. You're strange, it's all those self empowering workshops you go to.

TRUDY. Well it's an achievement to break up. Not everyone manages it. Most of us hang on in there to the bitter end, almost destroying each other.

GILL. Trudy I can't cope, with deep and meaningfuls so early in the morning. Pass me the skins.

TRUDY. It's two o' clock in the afternoon.

GILL. Who cares what the time is! Pass me the skins, and I'll build a big fat joint to go with brekky. You know where everything is?

TRUDY. I've brought everything including paper plates and cups.

> TRUDY *unfolds a paper tablecloth and puts it on the bed,*

unwraps fresh bagels, salmon and cream cheese. GILL *looks for her dope, searching her clothes while talking.*

GILL. I know we've been working at friendship for six months, but what's this in aid of? (*Gives up looking and takes half a joint from the ashtray on her dresser and passes it to* TRUDY.) Here, you light up.

TRUDY. No thanks. You got me into that shit. I'm trying to stop. I came round for an honest chat / you're the only person I feel safe speaking to.

GILL. I knew it –

TRUDY. Kat is up on her high horse, screaming black girls don't do SM, and my other mates refuse to talk about it.

GILL. I knew you had something else up your sleeve. Shit, where are the matches?

GILL *gives up looking and puts joint back in the ashtray.* TRUDY *passes her a bagel and takes one herself. They both take a bite.*

TRUDY. Please Gill, I'm serious. I've decided to play.

GILL. You what! (*Puts her bagel down on dresser.*)

TRUDY. Play, I want to explore and experiment with sex.

GILL. Great! What made you change your mind? This is worth celebrating. Where is the champagne?

TRUDY. I knew you would support me.

GILL. Does that mean we're back together again? Separation was definitely worth the angst.

TRUDY *puts her bagel down on the bed.*

TRUDY. Gill ... I want to play with Clio.

GILL. Oh, oh, I see, it's just that I thought maybe we would perhaps ...

Note: actors should play the following sequence up to page 74 as an intimate and physical scene, through contact, and use of voice/tone.

TRUDY. It's over between us as lovers. I've moved on.

GILL. Well I can see that. But are you sure? I mean, do you understand what you may be letting your self in for?

TRUDY. Not you too. I thought you would be the last person to be unsympathetic.

GILL. I'm sorry, it's just that ...

TRUDY. Just what?

GILL. Well you know ... I mean, you couldn't even cope with the thought of me using a dildo, or even using a dildo to penetrate me. Any time I mentioned whips, or scarfs, we argued. Sex toys cost me my relationship with you.

TRUDY. It's different.

GILL. How is it different?

TRUDY. We're both black.

GILL. What's that got to do with it?

TRUDY. I don't believe I'm going through the same shit with you six months later. I thought you understood the issues it brings up for me around race and power.

GILL. No! I don't understand, and I resent you assuming that I'm racist just because I'm white. As far as I'm concerned people like that hurt and offend others. Whenever the issue of SM comes up, why do we always end up down the same black hole?

TRUDY *gets up from the chair and points at* GILL.

TRUDY. 'Down the same black hole'! Did you hear what you just said? Down the same black hole you were happy to put your tongue down six months ago. You see, Gill, you've just hurt me. Your choice of language offends me.

GILL. Here we go again. Can't fuck with you in case my sexual preferences make you feel like a slave. Can't speak to you in case I offend you.

TRUDY. It's hard being close friends with a black woman, isn't it?

GILL. No it's just hard being friends with you.

TRUDY. When are you going to recognize I'm black and you're white?

GILL. When are you going to forget it?

TRUDY. When I can trust you.

GILL. Oh so you don't trust me now?

> TRUDY *sits down in a tense manner.*

TRUDY. I don't trust your conditioning. I don't trust what thoughts you may have in your head if we played together. I don't trust that you wouldn't get carried away while acting out a fantasy.

GILL. What the hell do you mean?

TRUDY. Calm down.

GILL. Calm down! You've got some bloody cheek, you come waltzing into my space to let me know you've got a new girl friend, and now you want me to listen to this crap.

TRUDY. I'm sorry.

GILL. Don't bother, why don't you leave and find some other white woman to guilt trip?

TRUDY. How can I make you understand, Gill? So many of black-white relationships in this society are based on the fact that black people have very little power. How do I know that when I give up my power to you in the bed, that you're not thinking 'nigger, slave, mugger'? And if you are, how do I know you won't play those thoughts out on my body?

GILL. But Trudy I could never think like that.

TRUDY. It's a risk I'm not prepared to take. What risks do you take, Gill?

GILL. I haven't thought about it.

TRUDY. Typical, you don't have to.

GILL. So you've made your point, but ...

TRUDY. Gill listen to me for a change. I know what you think.

GILL. Listen, how many times do I have to listen to the same tape?

TRUDY. I'm scared of all that bondage stuff, but when we spoke about it it did excite me. I'm not sure why, but every time I thought of you and I experimenting, I could hear my black sisters screaming, 'Remember slavery'.

GILL. What's this got to do with me, Trudy?

TRUDY. White people have got the power. They had the power and tortured my ancestors, in the same way people use bondage in sex. Shit I don't even have to go / back centuries.

GILL. Trudy, this is me Gill, the woman you made love with every day for a year. Ate off the same plate, shared our lives, and intimate secrets.

TRUDY. Exactly. When I fantasize about you handcuffing my hands, all I can think of is the police beating Michael White, gagging Joy Gardner to death and shooting Cherry Groce. The images, flashbacks and memories are endless.

GILL. How's all this stuff related to me Trudy? I love you.

TRUDY *breaks down in tears. Begins to unwind.*

TRUDY. That day.

GILL. What day?

TRUDY. I was fourteen, protesting against the Nazis marching in Southend, and the police picked on the only black person on the demo, arrested for not giving them my banner. They handcuffed me, slung me in the van, frisked me, and drove me to the station. Two women stripped me, forced me to bend over and touch my toes, and shoved their hands up my genitals.

GILL. Shit, why didn't you tell me?

TRUDY. They said it was a routine check. To make sure I had no dangerous weapons up there. (*Laughs to highlight how unbelievable it all seems.*)

GILL. Trudy, I know I was a copper. I don't think of the police beating up all the queers when I'm having sex, far from it. Look I understand your anger.

TRUDY. How dare you, no you don't understand, that's your problem.

GILL. But I do, I gave up my job for you.

TRUDY. You left because you couldn't cope with your colleagues bragging about how many poofs they had savagely beaten up, every night they went off duty. You couldn't cope pretending to be straight, you couldn't cope with how the force treated women when they reported rape, and when you started dating me, that was it, the overt racism was all too much.

GILL. God, it seems an age since I worked there, but you're right, they're things I choose to forget.

TRUDY. You have the luxury, the choice to forget. You've only started thinking about race since I've been in your life. You can't understand the best you can do is sympathise. You can never know what it's like to be a black person.

GILL. I suppose you're right.

TRUDY. How could I let you tie me up? How could l let you whip me? How could I? Those same whips were used to keep my ancestors at work on the plantations. My mother's and father's backs peeling raw, blood oozing, a tree trunk of slashes that can never be the same. I am the scar, my thoughts are still in pain.

GILL. I'm on fucking Ecstasy, not a bloody guilt trip.

TRUDY. Kat has a point.

GILL. Maybe she has, but when are you going to stop being a mouthpiece for her, and tell me what you really think?

TRUDY. How can I go out with somebody who triggers off all these memories? And to introduce whips, chains and handcuffs, is all too scarey to explore with a white woman. Especially my first time. I need to be able to trust, feel safe. Maybe I can feel safe with Clio.

GILL. But she was in a dog collar, and with a white woman Trace, holding Clio on a leash.

TRUDY. Clio obviously isn't a novice. And in any case she had all the power. The white woman was her slave.

GILL. I don't know what else to say.

TRUDY. You don't have to say anything. It's the first time you've heard me, and not got all defensive. I appreciate that, thank you.

> TRUDY *moves the bagels to the end of the bed, takes hold of* GILL *and they hug.* GILL *pulls away and looks into her eyes.*

GILL. What does this all mean? Can you never love a white woman?

TRUDY. Gill I love you. I wouldn't be here sharing my pain with you.

GILL. I love you too, but I'm confused, can you ever have a sexual relationship with a white woman?

TRUDY. I love women, all women, and I don't want to be caged by my legacy, but where I am at now in my healing, I want to explore with black women, but you know me, since I've been a lesbian I can't stop looking at women.

GILL.   I have a lot to think about. The irony is, that just as I've begun to question my sexual practices, you seem to be adopting them.

TRUDY.   No, I'm in a similar place as you. I'm just questioning and exploring my sexuality. You can't avoid it on the scene.

GILL.   Where's that healthy breakfast? I'm beginning to feel a bit rough. Where did I put that joint?

TRUDY.   There is something else.

GILL.   Oh no, not more d and ms (*i.e. 'deep and meaningfuls'*), I can't cope first thing in the morning.

TRUDY.   It's the afternoon for god sake. Some of us do get up to hear the morning chorus.

GILL.   Yeah, I've heard yours, thankyou very much. Now get a life.

TRUDY.   I'm trying to, champagne.

> TRUDY *pulls a bottle and two plastic glasses from her bag which is lying on the floor beside the chair. She shakes the bottle and loosens the cork.*

GILL.   Don't you dare.

TRUDY.   What's it worth?

GILL.   That depends.

TRUDY.   I want to borrow your equipment.

GILL.   What.

TRUDY.   You heard.

> TRUDY *passes* GILL *a glass, places part of sheet over cork and slowly pulls cork making sure nothing spills. She takes a bow and pours each of them a drink and puts bottle on dresser.*

TRUDY.   Cheers, to my sexual liberation.

> GILL *ignores the cheers, takes a sip and puts her glass down.*

GILL.   You don't even know her. Look, don't be coerced into anything you don't want to do.

TRUDY. I'm a big girl now.

GILL. Big or not, you don't even know what to do.

TRUDY. What makes you think that?

GILL. Go on, enlighten me

TRUDY. Well you know BD / likes to.

GILL. BD BD, not you too. That says it all. I've just listened to you harp out all that emotional stuff, and you have the audacity to mention BD. What an insult. At least I'm working on my racism / she's the biggest racist going.

TRUDY. Calm down, and it's not emotional, it's my reality. Just listen for a moment.

GILL (*in patois*). Kat will cuss your clart.

TRUDY. Cha so you tink your black now?

GILL. No, just wanted you to hear me too. I'm all ears for this one. Where's that joint?

TRUDY. Shouldn't think you'd need it.

GILL. Cut the crap. Get on with it.

TRUDY. BD's one of those white colonials.

GILL. As if I didn't know.

TRUDY. Don't make it hard for me.

GILL. Hard for you? What about me? She's one of those women you were talking about earlier, the ones with / fucked up fantasies.

TRUDY. Let me finish. She escaped the country because of politics.

GILL. Is that supposed to make me feel better? She is so racist it's unreal.

TRUDY. That's an understatement. She's one of those white women riddled with guilt, about what her ancestors / have done to Africa.

GILL. Ancestors! More like grandfathers, fathers and brothers. Cut the sob story, and give me the bare bones.

> BD *and* CLIO *enter, spotlight comes up creating a surreal cameo affect.* CLIO *walks round* BD *menacingly three times, with her rubber whip flexed over her shoulder,* BD *drops to her knees.*

TRUDY. Remember last year when all the barstaff used to complain that BD was favouring me, and pointed out it was obvious because I was the only black woman working there, that she was either scared of me, or being / tokenistic?

GILL. Out and out racist more like it. Yeah, I wondered how you felt about losing your special entitlements.

TRUDY. One night she hauled me into her office and broke down crying. Blabbering how sorry she was that things in South Africa hadn't seemed to have changed. She asked me to whip her as much as my ancestors had been beaten by her people.

GILL. And ...

TRUDY. I told her it would take me more than a life time. And she said, Perfect.

> CLIO *whips* BD *several times.* BD *gets turned on.* CLIO *pokes the handle of her whip in* BD*'s back.* BD *stands, and* CLIO *guides her off stage.*
> TRUDY *and* GILL *crack up laughing.*

GILL. Perfect! I can just imagine her. What a closet SM queen. She sounds well fucked.

TRUDY. Aren't we all?

GILL. Some more than others, obviously. Trudy, did you whip her?

TRUDY. Nope, I was waiting for that. Who do you take me for anyway?

GILL. I'm beginning to seriously wonder. But let's not get off the point, Trudy, what did you do?

TRUDY. Nothing. She used to send me all this kinky fetish under-wear, and letters with money. I didn't know who to tell or what to do, so I just kept it.

GILL. Everything?

TRUDY. Of course, her family is rich from diamonds.

GILL. That's politically incorrect.

TRUDY. Well, you didn't complain about the champagne dinners and presents.

GILL. You swine, you never told me

TRUDY. You never asked.

GILL. Those underwear you gave me in the past, were they from BD?

TRUDY. She's got good taste, hasn't she?

GILL. I don't believe you. You harp on to me about buying goods from South Africa, even though Nelson Mandela is free. Yet it's OK for you to take diamond money.

TRUDY. Oh, so working for the police is any better?

GILL. We all make mistakes.

TRUDY. You can say that again. So have I passed the test?

GILL. Maybe.

TRUDY. So where is the equipment?

GILL. Hold on, hold on, I don't remember saying yes. In fact I don't even remember you asking. What's it worth?

TRUDY. Sorry, ideologically unsound, remember?

GILL. You can do better than that. On your knees?

TRUDY. Are you sure?

GILL. What day did you say you were playing?

TRUDY. I didn't.

GILL. When are you going to start learning?

TRUDY. Not from you, that's for sure. I'm just here for the gear.

GILL. Who's a clever girl? Anyway, what did you want?

> *Note. The following part of this scene, up to and including the dildo sequence uses physical theatre and mime, and should last between 10-15 minutes.*
> GILL *pulls a small case from underneath her bed, picks it up and opens it.*

GILL. Have you made your mind up? You're not having the whole lot.

> TRUDY *begins to look uncomfortable.*

TRUDY. Oh you know, the usual, a harness, strap-on, and whip. Oh I don't know, you're the sexpert.

GILL *rummages through case.*

GILL. I suppose I better give you the smallest of what I've got. (*Pulls out a large black dildo.* TRUDY *almost jumps out of her skin.*)

TRUDY. That's the smallest?

GILL. Well you can have this one if you want. (*Pulls out a two foot pink double-ended dildo.*)

TRUDY. I'm not having that white thing dangling between my legs. You've gotta be joking.

GILL. Hope you're not being racist.

TRUDY. Look forget it, I can't go through with it.

GILL. Oh come on, I'm only teasing. But this one really is the smallest I've got. (*Takes hold of the black dildo again and throws it at* TRUDY.) Here, catch. (TRUDY *tries to catch it but drops it in embarrassment.* GILL *gets up and picks up dildo. Laughs.*) You really are a vanilla girl, if you get my drift.

TRUDY. Forget it. I'm going home.

GILL. Come over here. It's OK. All it is is a bit of dyed moulded rubber. Go on, touch it?

TRUDY *puts her hand out, and then pulls it away.*

TRUDY. It's so ugly.

GILL. This is Kat's favourite.

TRUDY. The *cow.* Kat uses a dildo! – she's never let on to me. You give me a hard time, but Kat can obviously help herself.

GILL. For a price. You'd be surprised to know what else your mentor gets up to.

TRUDY. I'm not interested. In fact I've had enough, I'm leaving.

GILL *grabs* TRUDY, *and puts her hand over her eyes.*

GILL. Trust me. Close your eyes, relax, and count up to a hundred. (*Straps a waist-and-leg harness and dildo onto* TRUDY, *over her trousers. Spins her around gently.*) You can open your eyes now.

TRUDY *nervously opens her eyes, looks straight ahead in fear.* GILL *pushes her towards the mirror.*

GILL. Go on look into the mirror.

> TRUDY *faces front stage, into imaginary mirror, and looks petrified. She looks down at the dildo very slowly and freezes. This and rest of dildo sequence is acted out in mime technique.*

GILL. Go on, move your hips a bit. Get comfortable, familiar. Get in touch with its power. Let the energy pulsate through your body.

> *While* GILL *talks,* TRUDY *begins to move her head and hand awkwardly towards dildo.* GILL *rummages in her case, finds a condom, and throws it towards* TRUDY.

GILL. Catch.

> TRUDY, *taken off guard, drops it and bends to discover what it is.*

GILL (*while* TRUDY *is bending*). Always wear one of these. Go on, you'll have to put it on yourself.

> TRUDY *gingerly opens the condom wrapper. She tries not to look at what she is doing.*

GILL. You're not an expert at this. You're going to have to look at what you're doing.

> TRUDY *looks down and diligently puts the condom on. As she rolls the condom down the dildo, she slowly becomes turned on. Engrossed with putting the condom on, her hips begin to gyrate.* GILL *snuggles up behind her and grabs her hands.*

TRUDY. How do I look?

GILL. Dare I say?

TRUDY. Oh go on, I trust your opinion.

GILL. Horny.

> *They burst out laughing. As they calm down they begin to gently move, falling into rhythm. They both appear to be turned on in a subtle manner.* GILL *begins to grope at* TRUDY *who responds, just as they are about to kiss.*
> *Sound of door bell ringing frantically.*
> *Instantly* TRUDY *pulls her knees together and tries to hide the dildo with her hands. She freezes with terror.* GILL *stands upright and turns to the door.*

GILL. Shit, the key! That's Kat, wait here. (*Exits and answers door.*)

GILL *re-enters with* KAT, TRUDY *still frozen.*

KAT. Ya alright sistah?

TRUDY. Yeah.

KAT. You don't look it. You look like your all knotted up in that coconut's dog lead. Can I give you a hand?

KAT *beckons towards* TRUDY *with her left hand, and then quickly grabs the handcuff with her right hand, pushing it up her sleeve. She throws a glance at* GILL.

TRUDY. No no, I'm alright. I just need the bathroom. (*Stands upright and bares all to* KAT.)

KAT. Bloodclart.

TRUDY *exits, rushing past* KAT *and* GILL.

KAT. You sell-out. So, we're into SM, are we?

GILL. You're a fine one to talk. What the hell has SM got to do with dildos?

TRUDY *re-enters, without harness and strap-on.*

TRUDY. Speaking of dildos, a little dicky-bird tells me I was wearing your favourite one.

KAT (*turns to* GILL). What have you two been gossiping about?

GILL. Me, gossip? As if ... My lips are sealed.

TRUDY. What else have you got tucked away in the closet, that you're trying to protect me from, Kat?

KAT. When are you going to learn that there are some things you don't discuss and do in front of white gals?

GILL. Great, but you fuck them.

TRUDY. What's that supposed to mean?

KAT. Nothing.

TRUDY. You're such a hypocrite.

KAT. Hush ya mout.

TRUDY. No I bloody won't. You give me a hard time about sleeping with white women, but it's alright for you to screw white girls, as long as nobody knows.

GILL. Oh so, I'm a secret am I?

TRUDY. Go on, worm your way out of this one.

KAT. So I slept with Gill, one night. What's the big deal?

TRUDY. I suppose you were drunk? You're the sell-out.

GILL. Look, if you girls don't mind continuing your fight outside, I've got a date tonight.

KAT. Key.

GILL. In the trunk.

> KAT *tries to move slowly around the room so that she can look into the trunk while keeping an ear on the conversation.*

TRUDY. Who with?

GILL. Never you mind.

TRUDY. You kept that under wraps.

GILL. You never gave me a chance. I've been listening to you all day. You've got what you need. Now leave, I need some space.

KAT. What's that all about? (*Sits on the bed, still trying to move closer to the trunk.*)

TRUDY. I'm having a scene with Clio.

KAT. Ratied, who ya tink you are, a Miss Whiplash?

TRUDY. Yes.

KAT. She a serious to bloodclart.

TRUDY. I'm fed up of your advice.

KAT. I thought you was a feminist?

TRUDY. I was christened a womanist and Zami when I met you.

KAT (*sucks teeth*). Same difference. Zamis don't do SM.

TRUDY. So what is Clio?

KAT. Well she ain't a Zami, that's for sure. Zamis are cultural women, who love women sexually and spiritually.

GILL. Anyone for a joint, bagels, champagne?

TRUDY *and* KAT *both scowl at her.*

GILL. Well, if you two are going to be miserable, I'll take the champers with me. (*Takes bottle and tries to put cork in. The others ignore her and continue their argument.*)

TRUDY. Clio is black / isn't she?

KAT. Black women don't / do SM.

TRUDY. Says who?

KAT. It's common knowledge.

TRUDY. Just like lesbianism is a white disease.

KAT. It's not in our genes. Clio must be one of those confused Americans.

TRUDY. Wrong! She's an Essex girl.

GILL. Look you two, if you don't mind, finish your conversation somewhere else. (*They both ignore* GILL*'s request.*)

KAT. How can you hang out with that woman? You saw her last night. She was acting out white master-black slave scenarios.

TRUDY. The white woman was her slave.

KAT. That's supposed to make it better? Next you'll be in a Hitler uniform brandishing swastikas, telling me it's alright, coz black people didn't kill Jews.

TRUDY. That is not true! What do you take me for? All I want to do is play. Explore pleasure, desire, fun. And if strapping a dildo on, wearing fetish gear, or playing with Clio is SM, so be it.

KAT. I'd rather you fucked with white women, than hang out with that bounty.

TRUDY. That's great, isn't it? You'd rather I fuck a black man than go out with white women, and fuck white women than go out with a black SM dyke. Anything else I need to know?

GILL. A girl can't even get peace in her own home.

KAT. I'm scared for you, Trudy. I don't want you to get corrupted. This SM is a total fuckup. It's not for black girls.

TRUDY. How can you say that?

KAT. Things are changing / admittedly but –

TRUDY. The only thing I can see what's changed is, years ago when you were my age, dykes seemed too frightened to talk about sex.

KAT. Maybe we were but we had politics.

GILL. Politics ... More like the fucking Gestapo.

TRUDY. So have I.

KAT. Promise me one thing. Please don't parade your sexual activities in public.

TRUDY. What, do it behind closed doors like you? (KAT *sucks teeth.*) Collude with the myth, pretend I don't like being overpowered, restrained, tied up?

KAT (*sucks teeth*). Girl, you too damn English.

GILL. Trudy, you've got my keys, lock up, I've had enough. This is worse than a fucking acid trip.

KAT. Gill, the key!

GILL. They're in the trunk.

> GILL *exits.*

TRUDY. Key, what key? Don't say you've got keys to Gill's flat as well?

KAT. No, just me need a key.

TRUDY. For what?

KAT. Nothing man, it alright. (*Moves toward the trunk and stretches to enter it.*)

TRUDY (*pointing to* KAT). Handcuff! (KAT *sits upright and grabs hold of her wrist.*)

KAT. Yeah man, I can explain.

TRUDY. I'm sure you can. Next you'll be telling me that your Mrs has to keep you on a dog lead because she can't trust you.

KAT. It's not like that honest.

TRUDY. Oh, so you got arrested, and escaped from police custody.

KAT. Gill, me a kill your pussyclart.

TRUDY. Leave Gill out of this.

KAT. Give me a squeeze.

TRUDY. A squeeze! I can't take no more.

KAT. Me sorry, me know what oona must be thinking.

TRUDY. Cut the patois, I've had it up to here with you and your sermons.

KAT. What's your problem?

TRUDY. My problem! How fucking dare you, you've got more front than Brigitte Bardot.

KAT. Ophrah Winfrey, to be exact.

TRUDY. Is that supposed to be politically aware? (*Looks at her watch.*) Shit is that the time? I'm covering for you tonight. If I had known it was because of this, I would have said No.

KAT. I'm going for an interview.

TRUDY. Can't you take the pace?

KAT. I'm just fed up of having to work my butt off in the bar and earning extra cash teasing BD. Come on, Trudy, you know the score. You wasn't interested in BD's offer so I jumped in while the fire was hot. It was either that or live on the streets.

TRUDY. Some of us have politics.

KAT. Yes me dear, you nah see it.

TRUDY. I'm serious Kat, I need to think, I respected you and your opinions, but now, I just don't know who to listen to anymore.

> TRUDY *and* KAT *exit.*
> *Black out.*

Scene Five

Diva's Bar.
Disco lights are flashing, trance music is pumping.
CLIO *enters with* BD *and her slave* TRACE, *both in dog collars.* CLIO *walks as if she is riding in a chariot, with* BD *and* TRACE *pulling her along.* TRUDY *enters the bar and does a double take. She switches the light on.*

TRUDY. What the hell is going on here? Not you too?

CLIO. I've found meself another slave.

TRUDY. A what?

CLIO. Isn't she a good girl? She's done all the cleaning for yer.

TRUDY. Including the toilets?

CLIO. Everything. What else would you like er to do? This is your night off.

TRUDY. Nothing.

CLIO. Watch me. Turn, you son of a bitch. (BD *is on all fours. She turns to face* CLIO *with head towards the floor.*) Lick my boots. (TRACE *prepares the boot, caressing it with her face.* CLIO *yanks her by the collar to bid her stop.* BD *seductively licks both boots.* CLIO *pulls* BD's *head up and spits in her face.* TRACE *is jealous.*) You've left a mark. (TRACE *pushes* BD *out of the way and licks the boot.*) Good girl.

TRUDY. Stop ! Let them go, it's horrible. (BD, TRACE *and* CLIO *stop.*)

CLIO. What do you think, BD?

BD. Wonderful, absolutely wonderful.

CLIO. Why don't you join us? BD would love yer too.

TRUDY. No / no –

CLIO. It's fine, I know everything. BD and I ave ad a long talk, setting out the ground rules.

TRUDY. I'm not interested, in fact I'm handing in my notice as of now.

CLIO. Easy easy babe, I've just earnt you a night off work.

TRUDY. I can't take any more, lesbians are screwed up like everybody else.

CLIO *pulls the leash, and cracks a whip on the floor.*

CLIO. Time's up, BD, Trudy and I ave got things to talk about.

BD *exits on all fours,* TRACE *takes hold of the leash and leads her off.* CLIO *drops whip to the floor and tries to embrace* TRUDY *who pulls back.*

TRUDY. There's nothing to talk about, I've had enough.

CLIO. Oh come on babe, I've just earnt you a night off from that mother fucker, don't bottle out now.

TRUDY. That was repulsive, it's no different when the roles are reversed either.

CLIO. It's just a game, I'm only giving BD what she wants. It's the only kind of sex she knows.

TRUDY. You call that sex?

CLIO. Well there's sex and sex, babe. I own Trace, she's my slave. But it's you I wanna make love to.

TRUDY. Clio, I just don't know, I need time to think, you and Trace are such a contradiction. I can't cope with it all. Maybe I'll meet with you in the bar, for half an hour when Kat shows up.

CLIO. It's a date.

TRUDY. Half an hour, and then I'm going to have the evening all to myself.

CLIO. Be-ave. (*Begins to exit.*)

TRUDY (*picks up whip and throws it at* CLIO*'s feet*). You've forgotten something.

CLIO. Why thankyou, mam. (*Takes a bow.*)

TRUDY. You're impossible.

CLIO *exits.* TRUDY *walks to the bar and begins setting up for the night.* TRACE *enters.*

TRUDY. Hi Trace, what are you doing back here?

TRACE. I thought I'd grab a drink.

TRUDY. Sorry, we're closed.

TRACE. Not even a little one?

TRUDY. Just this once, don't make it a habit. (*Gives her a drink and continues to stock check.*)

TRACE. Are you OK?

TRUDY. No I'm not, I feel as if I'm going mad, I thought I was a lesbian until I began working here. Are you dating Clio?

TRACE. Believe me, Trudy, all I do is serve my mistress. I belong to everyone and no one.

TRUDY. Did you go home with that gay guy last night?

TRACE. Why?

> GILL *enters and walks up to the bar.*

TRUDY. I thought you were a dyke?

GILL. Yeah, so did I.

TRACE. I am, I just happen to get a thrill showing those faggots who really did invent penetration.

GILL (*sarcastic*). Oh, you're so cool.

TRACE. Right, I suppose it's time for me to go, tell Kat I'll pop by tomorrow.

TRUDY. Seeyah.

> TRACE *exits.*

TRUDY. You don't have to be so nasty.

GILL. She just gives me the creeps.

TRUDY. Each to their own.

GILL. Did Kat find the key?

TRUDY. I'm not interested.

GILL. Hasn't she explained?

TRUDY. You heard.

GILL. Oh come on it's not as bad as you think.

TRUDY. Has she asked you to try and butter me up?

GILL. No, but I know for a fact, Kat may be hypocritical at times, but she's not into bondage, that's for sure. She's got politics –

TRUDY. Oh, and I haven't?

GILL. I know how you must feel.

TRUDY. Tell me, because I don't.

GILL. Betrayed, but chill out a bit, and when you're ready give her a chance, she believes in you.

> KAT *enters looking smug.*

TRUDY. I believed in her once.

KAT. Got the job girls.

GILL. Doing what?

KAT. Working nights in a refuge hostel, the money is brilliant.

> BD *walks out of her office, having changed out of bondage gear.*

BD. So what's the celebration?

KAT. It's my last night in this hole.

BD. Well right now you're still an employee of mine, let's see some action. Kat, Gill, everything needs cleaning tonight. I've got the inspectors in tomorrow morning. We're opening an hour later.

GILL. What about Trudy?

BD. She's on a date tonight. (TRUDY *joins others at the bar. To* TRUDY.) Go on then, what are you waiting for? It's your night off.

KAT. Date?

GILL. Who with?

TRUDY. Nobody, I'm just having a quick drink with Clio.

BD. Enough chat, I want to see your beautiful teeth sparkling on the glasses.

> KAT *sucks teeth and mutters.* BD *exits into office.* TRUDY *pours two glasses of water and sits at the table.* GILL *takes a coin from her back pocket and flips it. She catches it and puts both clenched fists out in front of* KAT. *Coin is concealed in left hand.*

GILL. Tails – waitress, heads – bar dyke.

> KAT *taps the left fist.* GILL *seductively opens her fist and tails appears.* GILL *smiles.*

GILL. I've always wanted to see you in a mini.

KAT. Cha, me stay right here.

GILL. Spoil-sport.

> CLIO *walks in, dressed in club-style trousers, T-shirt, and baseball cap, and a studded dog collar round her neck. She has a full-size leather mistress whip. She saunters up to* TRUDY's *table and sits down. They look apprehensive of each other.*

KAT. Me can't stand that woman.

GILL. What has she done to you?

KAT. She's into sado-masochism and that stinks.

GILL. What's wrong with consensual sex?

KAT. What's consensual about being tied up, pierced, being whipped?

GILL. Oh come on, stretch your imagination, would you let me tie you up?

KAT. No what you take me for?

GILL. Precisely, if you want it you get it.

KAT. Me nah care, what's consensual about her?

GILL. You mean Clio? She's a work of art, she's stunning.

KAT. You might score good weed, but that's as far as it goes. SM is violence, end of story.

GILL. New story, if violence happens in an SM relationship that's abuse. Your last relationship was violent, you and Kya used to knock the shit out of each other. When you confided in me you realised you didn't have to stay with each other. If I was into violence, I would have said, Great, stay, enjoy the party. You know how concerned I was. I couldn't even get advice from friends, through fear of being called racist. Instead I laid awake every night wondering if you would be alive the next time we met.

KAT. That's different. You'll never convince me that SM is not violence. I've seen it all in here, whip marks, knife slashes, piercings.

> TRUDY *walks up to the bar.*

TRUDY. You two look intense. Hey Clio says BD's cleaned the place from top to bottom.

KAT. And how would she know that?

TRUDY. She's got a name, why don't you ask her?

KAT. Cha she's got attitude to rasclart.

TRUDY. And you haven't?

KAT. Let's talk.

TRUDY. Not now, I'm on holiday.

GILL. We better check the cellar is clean.

KAT. I'll ring.

TRUDY. I've got an answering machine. Two Beck's, please.

KAT. I'm sorry Ms Ting, we're busy cleaning.

> GILL *and* KAT *exit.* TRUDY *takes two Beck's from the bar and sits back down with* CLIO. *She raises her hand and seductively runs it along* CLIO's *collar. The rest of the scene to the end of the play should have a sense of unreality, aided by use of lighting to denote a private space.*

TRUDY. I absolutely adore this.

CLIO. Really, it's a relic from my Ell's Angel days.

TRUDY. You a Hell's Angel? I've heard it all now.

CLIO. Why are you so surprised? I still wear most of the same clothes as I did then.

TRUDY. I've always wanted to be a punk with pink and green hair.

CLIO. What's stopping you?

TRUDY. They're out of fashion now, silly.

CLIO. Why don't you come ome with me?

TRUDY. I'm scared.

CLIO. You can trust me.

TRUDY. How can I? I don't even know you. I thought I could trust Kat.

CLIO. It doesn't matter, as long as you can trust yourself, the magic word is 'Stop'.

TRUDY. How do I know you will stop? How can I trust you?

You come gatecrashing into my workplace, shocking the living daylights out of everybody.

CLIO. That's coz I'm black.

TRUDY. It was because you were on a dog lead.

CLIO. I'm sorry, I just wanted to surprise you.

TRUDY. Well, you managed that.

CLIO. I thought you andled me very well. I can't stop thinking about yer.

TRUDY. I said I'm scared, Clio.

CLIO. Why?

TRUDY. You, BD and your slave, it gives me the creeps, but part of you excites me. I've never felt so charged before.

CLIO. Can you name it? What are you feeling?

TRUDY. All I know is that the same thing which turns me on, is the same thing which scares me. You push my boundaries, press my buttons, and I just hate feeling out of control.

CLIO. But you can always be in control if we talk about sex first. Talk about what we will do and what we won't. That is the exciting thing about sex, talking, exploring fantasies. Acting out what we feel comfortable with.

TRUDY. I can't, black girls don't do your type of sex.

CLIO. Be-ave. What am I? A snowflake in disguise? Sounds like your girlfriends ave given yer a right grilling.

TRUDY. You are different.

CLIO. The only difference is that I don't pretend. I sleep with who I want to. I ave great difficulty pretending I'm not on eat just because the woman is the wrong colour, or size. And I've ad my fair share of black girls who ave taught me a thing or two.

TRUDY. I didn't mean to say that. I know it's a stupid comment.

CLIO. Come on, let's play a little. Ead fucking gives me chronic migraine.

TRUDY. No, I hate those bondage games. You and BD ... Yuck.

CLIO. Ow about some magic? (*She takes a bow and pulls out a hanky from under her collar. She entrances* TRUDY *seductively with the hankies during the following.)*

TRUDY. You're always playing with hankies, what does that mean?

CLIO. I'm appy to take either role tonight. (*Clenches her left hand into a fist and stuffs the hanky down it. She blows into her fist like a conjurer and beckons* TRUDY *to do the same.*) It's your treat, you pull. (TRUDY *begins pulling from the fist and a white hanky appears.*) Um, a girl who knows what she wants, you'll do both of us, will yer? (TRUDY *giggles, and pulls again, a mauve one appears.*) Um, naval fetish.

> TRUDY *begins to pull quickly and several coloured hankies appear.* CLIO *grabs the string of hankies tight. She waves the last colour – yellow – at* TRUDY *and laughs.*

TRUDY. My favourite colour.

CLIO. What, water sports?

TRUDY. I love anything to do with water. (*Spins into* CLIO'*s arms, bound by the hankies.*)

CLIO. Not this type, surely? Even I can't cope with yellow ankies babe.

TRUDY. You're frightening me. (*Pulls away, and the hankies fall to the floor.*)

CLIO. So name your game. What's your fantasy? Lighten up.

> *This rest of the scene is acted in physical theatre style.*
> TRUDY *smiles. She does a cart-wheel.*

CLIO. Oh no, none of that fancy stuff.

> TRUDY *continues to act physical, farcically, egging* CLIO *on. She stands upright all of a sudden and pushes her chest out. She starts beating on her chest.*

TRUDY (*Tarzan call*). Me Tarzan.

CLIO (*with surprise*). Me Jane, be-ave.

TRUDY. Why not?

> *They act out a short Tarzan-Jane skit.* CLIO *breaks the fun.*

CLIO. I'm Samson and you're Delilah.

They act a short Samson and Delilah skit. TRUDY *breaks the fun.*

TRUDY. I'm Romeo and you're Juliet.

CLIO. 'Slowly and wise, they stumble who run fast.'

TRUDY. Thumbelina, all the better to fuck you with.

CLIO (*gasps*). I'm Sleeping Beauty.

TRUDY. King Kong. (*Walks in a King Kong style towards his Sleeping Beauty.*)

CLIO (*screams*). Take me, take me, I'm Alice in Wonderland. (*Moves in slow motion, showing her delight at seeing* TRUDY, *exuding sexuality. She gently takes her hand, hair, and reacts with delight.* TRUDY *begins to feel awkward from the attention.*) *

TRUDY. I'm Tom.

CLIO. I'm Jerry.

> *They take turns to act out Tom and Jerry. They play with the whip, sexualizing, using it as their tail, snatching the whip off each other.* CLIO *is excited and gets carried away as Tom.* TRUDY *becomes excited too as Jerry, she stands up on two legs and roars like a lion.* CLIO *picks up the whip and acts as a ring leader. They act out this scene.* TRUDY *grabs hold of the whip and begins to crack it. She becomes intoxicated by its power. They pull the whip from each other, cracking the floor with it.* CLIO *remains sexual in her whipping style, while* TRUDY *becomes excited, dangerous, out of control, unsafe, going beyond boundaries. She begins to crack the whip at* CLIO *and becomes more and more excited and carried away.*

CLIO. Stop!

> *Instant blackout.*

SECTION FOUR

QUEENIE COMES TO TOWN

BORN TO BE A QUEEN

When I came to town, I came in female form cloaked in a black skin. Born to be a Queen, I wasn't prepared for society's stigma towards my colour, gender, race, sexuality, culture and attitudes. But by the time I evolved into Queenie I was well sussed.

Named Valerie Jane Mason-John at birth, renamed Queenie twenty-eight years later by gay men living in San Francisco, because they decided I was a bigger Queen than all of them hanging out in the Castro. And they were right.

It took another five years to rediscover that true aristocratic self which so many of us black people left behind in our countries of origin. Due to colonial racism, many of us are constrained to live in a class lower than our real one and denied our true social status amidst the many struggles we are faced with to survive in Britain.

THE COLOUR OF MY SKIN

The colour of my skin is the root of my ecstasy
The seed of my life
The colour of my skin is one of nature's glories
The bloom of my life

The colour of my skin is the flower of my legacy
The taboo of my oppressors
The colour of my skin is the greatness of my beauty
The guilt of my kidnappers

The colour of my skin is the celebration of Eden
Black is an omnipotent being
The rejoicing of life
Black the colour of many skins
Is nature's own deliberation

The colour of my skin is your wonder
My pleasure
Your fear
My strength, my beauty

INGLAN IS A BITCH

1998 is the commemorative year of the Windrush, the first boat to bring black workers from the Caribbean to England, and some people in the black community are celebrating. I say, what is there to celebrate? It's just part of the fleet which brought the first slaves from Africa to England five hundred years ago.

'It is different,' argued Philippa Gregory (author of 'A *Respectable Trade*' and the serialised drama of the same name shown on BBC television in Spring 1998), during a discussion with me on the James Whale radio show, because in her view the people who came to England 50 years ago weren't given a one way ticket: 'They could return if they didn't like it.'

However, many of these people who came to England in the 40s, 50s and 60s are descendants of the slaves who were pillaged from Africa and brought to work on the Caribbean plantations, or to work as household servants, prostitutes, or for the sexual convenience of privileged Englishmen. Five hundred years later, people of African descent were brought in 1948 to work in low paid jobs in the National Health Service and on London Transport. The main differences were we weren't flogged to death or treated as barbaric savages.

But we still are the most vulnerable group on the streets with regard to police harassment and brutality, and it has been said by indigenous Australians and black Americans that black people throughout the world are the most institutionalised race in the criminal justice and the mental health systems. In 1998 the Commission for Racial Equality cited the following: that black people are eight times more likely to be stopped and searched than white people; that there is one incident of racial harassment or abuse every four minutes; that for every attack on a white person there are eight on Afro-Caribbeans and sixteen on Pakistanis; and that according to some reports, ethnic minorities receive prison sentences up to nine months longer than white people up on identical charges.

WINDRUSH

They say she was pregnant,
Came to sea full of me
Weighing her down in shoes dem
Baggy and all

They say the ship nearly sink
Me mudda never sleep a wink
They say Inglan full of promise
All my mudda do is reminisce

A stowaway she was
Hidden between the trunks
But she came
Coz my poppa came
She was full of me
And I was gonna make her rich

Her tummy bulging,
Sea sick,
Morning sick,
Home sick.

She had heard London streets
Were paved with gold
But what kinda nancy story was dis?
Obia playing his tricks
Me mudda and poppa feeling his licks

London streets are paved with sleet
Me mudda cried every night,
And me granny wrote back,
I thought you sailed on the Goldrush
No Granny, the Windrush
And the streets are paved with sleet.

Sleet what dat?
Some kinda fancy name for your man
Granny wrote back.

I arrived on the dot,
What happened to black fella time?
Me mudda ask the nurse,
Me poppa sneered,
Inglan is a bitch

This was Inglan's crime
No rice n peas
No stew pot or dumplings
No ackee n salt fish
No cassava leaf

But me mudder and poppa survived
Malnutrition
Humiliation
Integration

Welcome to the land of honey and milk
The posters said back home
Sweet honey and money
Obia playing his tricks
Giving me mudda and poppa his licks

But their baby gonna be all right
Me mudda still curse,
And me granny too
The only gold she see when she visit Inglan
Was gold pon me poppa's teeth
And tea what dat?
Where the bush tea? gunja tea?

But me mudda still sing to me every night
Cooing in my ear
All her babies gonna be all right
Despite
the
night
she
set
sail

pon
the
Windrush

What dat some fancy name you give your man?

YES OFFICER

Good evening all
Yes officer

I've been watching you
Yes officer

Been here long?
Yes officer

Loitering are we?
Yes officer

Not hot enough?
Yes officer

Been to the jungle bar?
Yes officer

Drunk on jungle juice?
Yes officer

Bloody coon, it's only noon
Yes officer

What are you looking at?
Yes officer

Empty your pockets
Yes officer

That's property of Brixton Market
Yes officer

Drop those bananas now
Yes officer

Under arrest for armed robbery
Yes officer

Got a name, have you?
Yes officer

How old are you?
Yes officer

Do you have papers?
Yes officer

Can I see them?
Yes officer

That's assault
Yes officer

You're nicked
Yes officer.

Things have changed since we arrived en masse fifty years ago, but as black people we still experience racism every day of our lives. When I'm asked by white lesbians, what is more important, my race or sexuality, I say, how can I deny my racial identity, when aged six, white ladies came running up to my white house mother in the high street, screaming how disgusting she was for having a mongrel?

WHICH YEAR WAS IT?

I'm six years old
female and black,
sitting in classroom
listening to my teacher
tell me about the world
and all its colourful people.

"Africans and Aborigines
are the evolutionary link
between man and monkey.
They swing from trees
and are cannibals."

I'm seven years old
listening to my transistor
which Santa brought me for Christmas.
A man tells a story of a black girl
who bathed in a bath of bleach.
I'm disturbed.
Twenty three years later
I learn I too was
trying to bleach my skin white
before the age of four.

I'm eight years old
my village school
has closed down.
My first day at
a new school
I'm sent home.
I punch a boy
for calling me a wog.

I'm nine years old,
and talking to a white lady.
I use my hands to express myself,
she screams,
"Ooh hands just like monkeys."

I'm ten years old
and I want to be
Sleeping Beauty.

My teachers says no,
because she wasn't black.
I'm given the role of
manoeuvring the spotlight
for the whole show.

I'm eleven years old
attending a secondary school
in London.
I want to take up a second
instrument, the oboe
I have several tries at blowing,
my music teacher says I can't
make a tune,
because my lips are too big.

I'm twelve years old
distressed by having
to think about my race
but I have no choice.

I'm thirty one years old
sunning my body
at Hampstead ladies pond
with other black girls.

A life guard comes to join us,
she informs us that black people
can't swim properly
because of our hips.
We laugh and take a dip.

BROWN GIRL IN THE RING

Performance Piece for Solo Actor

NOTE: '*Brown Girl in the Ring*' was inspired by a workshop with the American Actor/Director and Co-founder of the international touring company *Sprit Britches*, Lois Weaver.

She instructed us to bring in a picture of our family. So instead of falling into negative mental states about not having a biological family, I looked at a picture of a jigsaw puzzle showing a group of white French aristocrats at a ball and decided this was my family. After all, as a Barnardo child I socialised regularly with the royal, the rich, the famous, at parties and events thrown annually. I wrote a 15-minute piece, called '*Sweep it Under the Carpet*', which I performed as 'Queenie' as part of the workshop's one-night event at Jackson's Lane Community Theatre in December 1996, and also as part of the Apple and Snakes Comedy Night at the Battersea Arts Centre in Spring 1997.

The response to the piece encouraged me to develop it further, but only after I had plucked up the courage to perform a one-woman show. The piece was further developed by Britain's leading Black theatre company Talawa (guided by Yvonne Brewster and Greta Mendez), for their 'Zebra Crossing 2' season at the Lyric Studio Hammersmith for eight performances in October/November 1998. A full length one woman show, directed by Paul Everitt and produced by Jennifer Dean, opened at the Oval House Theatre, London, for three weeks in January 1999 before touring other major cities.

The cast was as follows:

REGINA .... Queenie

The text here is the 'Lyric' version. Those wanting to stage the 'Oval' version, please contact the author.

Sponsors for the Oval production included: Jennifer Dean, Oval House, Talawa, Pink Paper and the Glass Bar.

I dedicate my show to my children's home sister, lover, best friend, all bound up in one. When I think of you, I think of the record 'Brown Girl in the Ring', and of the following.

REMEMBER

Remember when we lived country and we used to go raving in those awful discos? And surprise surprise the record 'Brown Girl in the Ring' just happened to be playing out aloud over the speakers as we walked on to the dance floor, while handbags were swiftly pulled away by petrified white girls who feared we might steal their belongings. We showed them who 'The Brown Girls in the Ring' really were when the record 'Everybody was Kung Fu Fighting' came on, by attracting an audience with our dancing talents. Once the music became dry, we could never leave due to the queue of people wanting our signature. You were so good at doing American accents, that we became even more exotic, lapping up every minute of it.

Remember when your big sister introduced us to the 'ruffneck' night life of shabeams, and blues. The Bronx, the Cemetry, Chickens and Hideaway became our favourites. We'd harass the poor DJ for soul or funk all night long. No matter which shabeam we were at, the DJs all seem to give in at 6 am and play 'Freak Out'. Which gave us permission to show them that these two brown girls freely dancing the night away, with posh English accents, were aliens from out of town.

Remember when you left your boyfriend Tony and I left my girl friend Chris and we went travelling the world, hitch-hiking from Israel, to Greece, to Turkey, through Western Europe and home. People always thought you were a native of their country, well until we arrived in Germany, and then you must have arrived on a boat from Africa with me. Nobody ever believed we came from England, they just looked and nodded, dictating Americano, Africano, no blacks in England.

Remember that man on Dam Square in Amsterdam who asked us where we came from? And I replied, Japan. We really did become 'Brown Girls in the Ring', cameras flashed, fingers wagged.

Remember when people thought I was Joan Armatrading, Grace Jones and Tracy Chapman. And you were mad because I could have made us some money by forging their signature. Well just for you sister, so fed up of being abused in Australia for being an unfriendly film star, I finally gave in and forged Whoopi Goldberg's name. Remember your dare, well I did it, I told a taxi driver in Australia that I had swung from trees and swam the ocean to reach Australia, and bless his cotton socks, he believed me. Remember you owe me a thousand pounds for that one.

And now you really are the 'Brown Girl in the Ring', lost to the drug of the millenium. One day, we'll party again, on that thousand pounds you owe me remember!

THE PLAY: BROWN GIRL IN THE RING

On stage is a throne constructed like a jigsaw and jigsaw pieces on the floor.

On the backdrop is projected a picture of a white royal-looking family. One of the female figures' heads is missing.

Audience is seated. Spotlight comes up on auditorium exit/entrance.

A music box version of Beethoven's 'Für Elise' is playing. REGINA *enters from auditorium, wearing a ballet dress with several petticoats underneath, bloomers, ballet shoes, a Georgian white powdered courtier's wig and jewels fit for a queen. She walks in on tiptoe holding a champagne glass in one hand and an imaginary dance partner in the other. She pirouettes facing the throne. She points with her right foot in front of her left and behind. She pirouettes gracefully, leaps into the air several times using the cabriole position. On landing she moves into her first arabesque (like a graceful version of the yoga position: the tree). She pirouettes on one foot in this position as if to reach and touch one side of the audience with her hand and the other side with her foot. Coming out of this position she performs the Dying Swan. She gracefully stands and does ballet bows to the audience. She is in her element. Throughout she has held onto the champagne glass, now she holds it as if it were a magnificent bouquet of flowers. She gracefully walks to the throne and sits. She strikes a pose, then another and finally a third before becoming completely still, observing her guests (the audience). Throughout the monologue she always moves in a highly stylised fashion, speaking in an exaggerated upper class English aristobratish voice.*

REGINA. Waiter, Waiter, Wait ... Wait ...

On the abrupt impulse of 'Wait ...' she sits back into her throne. She speaks as if she is in conversation with the waiter.

Wait!

Champagne glass goes flying.

Oh how stupid of me. Sweep it under the carpet.

She looks up.

At long last

Yes, most perfunctory
I'll have caviar ... and rice and peas
I said, Caviar ... and rice and peas
How dare you question me?
No I'm not mistaken
Caviar ... and rice and peas
I had hashish for starters
Exotic, um lychees will be absolutely marvellous for dessert
Oh waiter would you be so kind as to switch the air conditioning
    on when you return to your menial tasks.
I beg your pardon
Oh used to the heat, yes, yes of course Australia was absolutely
    divine last month.
Aborigine?
No no, you don't quite understand. I am as English as Her Majesty.
My title is Regina
Not vagina, Regina
W!O!G! My poor poppet you do seem to be losing it.
I am most definitely not a Western Oriental Gentlemen.

Chip, chip, chip. On my shoulder? Which chip? On my shoulder,
    chip, raining chips.
But it only rains cats and dogs in England.
Now scarper, enough of your verbal bowel syndrome
I have friends to attend to.
Now where was I?

> REGINA *slowly regresses in her throne and begins to sing in an*
> *eight-year-old's voice. She explores the throne by turning upside*
> *down in it.*

(*Sings.*) *'There's a brown girl in the ring*
    Tra la la la la
    There's a brown girl in the ring
    Tra la la la la la
    Brown girl in the ring
    Tra la la la la'

I look like the sugar
In the plum plum plum

Speaking in the eight-year-old's voice.

My mummy says I'm special
She says I look like the
Sugar in the plum plum plum

> *Bends her head back and raises her right hand in front of her eyes, contorting her fingers into an irregular shape. She begins speaking to her imaginary friend.*

What do you think Lizard?
Sticks and stones will break your bones
But names will never hurt you – really Lizard, really

> *Leaps off the throne with right hand still contorted and skips. Begins to play with the jigsaw pieces on the floor while still chanting her mantra to the audience.*

Sticks and stones will break your bones
And names will never hurt me

> *Builds a table out of the jigsaw pieces.*

Really, really Lizard, Really

> *Sits on floor at the table and plays with her petticoats. She counts each petticoat.*

One, two, three, four, five.

> *As she becomes aware of the audience she becomes adult again.*

My shrink says they're good for catching the flies with
Oh indeed he cost me Buckingham Palace
Of course my sweeties, you're all here to observe
The family's heirloom.

> *Walks to her throne, takes a regal pose and begins to pout a little, as if she were having her photo taken. Begins to shrink herself in the throne by becoming smaller. Suddenly breaks out into song, singing like an eight-year-old.*

(*Sings.*) 'There's a brown girl in the ring', etc.

I look like the fly
In the milk, milk, milk.

> *By the end of the song she is crouching in her throne.*

As she calls out each name following she becomes bigger, standing on the throne by the time she calls the last one.

Kunte Kinte
Chicken George
Martin Luther King
Malcolm X
Muhammad Ali
Marcus Garvey
Bob Marley

Sweep it under the carpet

Now you see I descend from a royal lineage of Africans who were captured and brought to France in the 16th century. Indeed they remained very proud. So much so that they couldn't quite understand why my Great Great Grand Dadada was affected by the paler complexion, Lily Whites so to speak. The poor man brought a curse upon the family by impregnating a Persil White, a, a, a, Daz White a, a, a, Tampax White a, a, a, Lily White. And that was the last we heard of the natives.

Sweep it under the carpet.

My Great Great Grand Mamama from the Dom Perignon family was married off to the family queer, and packed off to England to raise her predicament in secret. When my Great Grand Mamama was 18 she was also betrothed to the next family queer in line, in the hope of erasing the primitive strain.

> *She sweeps her petticoats up, masking her face. As she sweeps them up:*

Sweep it under the carpet.

> *Calls for her imaginary friend Lizard in a child's voice, still hiding behind petticoats.*

Lizard, Lizard, Lizard,
You can't see me
Boo

> *Pulls petticoats away from her face and continues to play with them.*

You can't see me
Boo

> *Jumps off the throne. Sings in a child's voice doing a little dance with the petticoats to go with the song.*

(*Sings.*) 'There's a brown girl in the ring', etc.

I look like the currant
In the hot cross bun, bun, bun.

> *Becomes so excited she knocks table over, and becomes the adult again.*

Sweep it under the carpet.

Accidents do happen: yes by some idiosyncratic malfunction they produced a fine specimen of a daughter, red curly hair and green eyes. They named her The Pink Lady. She looked so respectable, she was married off into a notable family. The Lansons of Monte Carlo. And between the two of them they produced four boys and one girl.

My Mamama, she is claimed to be the most beautiful lady in Champagne.

> *Pirouettes, showing herself off, as if she were her Mamama.*

Accepted back into the Domperignon family, she was brought back to France, and betrothed to my Dadada Moët et Chandon. Oh indeed it was a splendid wedding, masquerading for seven days and seven nights, and in the Fall my Mamama fell pregnant, and in the Summer she gave birth.

> *Pauses, and looks at the picture as if seeing it for the first time. Recoils.*

Throw back!

> *Turns to the imaginary waiter.*

No not you, you fool,
Sweep it under the carpet

> *Turns to face picture with her back to the audience. On each phrase she turns to face audience then back to picture, building up into a frenzy.*

Throw back, throw back, throw back, back, back, back,
Waiter, I'm technophobic, throw back, throw back, throw back
No I don't want reggae music, throw back, throw back, throw back
I was quite happy listening to Handel's 'Messiah', you toe rag.

> *Reaching a climax in her movement she spins, and the movement brings her back to her senses.*

Now where was I?

> *She pauses as if she were going to burst into song.*

Well out popped my twin brother, blonde hair and blue eyes,
Laurent Perrier Chandon
And five minutes later out ...
Hallelujah, Hallelujah, Hallelujah

Waiter, my guests are still seated,
Why aren't they standing?

> *Sound of Hallelujah chorus from Handel's 'Messiah' blasts out.*
> REGINA *acts as conductor to the audience.*
> *Conducts audience to stand. Leaves stage and walks back down the aisle smiling as if she were the Queen. She takes her place on the throne. Music begins to fade.*

And out popped me.

> *Music stops.*
> *Bursts into hysterical laughter, trying to speak at the same time.*

My poor Mamama never spoke again and Dadada castrated himself.
I was packed off to family friends in England, the Bollys of Ascot.

> *Sits back in throne, trying to subtly arrange herself.*

They were very kind to me, they civilised me, taught me etiquette, deportment lessons. But the problem began when they sent me to the family doctor, for my apparent skin condition. He in turn sent me to the family psychiatrist, who suggested I re-create my family picture.

> *Gets up from throne and walks to jigsaw pieces. Takes hold of one jigsaw piece on the floor and looks at it as if it were a mirror.*

So that night I tore out a page from the Bollys' album, and where there were heads cut out, I pasted in pictures like me from a native book I acquired as a child.

Strange, that!

> *Places jigsaw piece over her head, as if she is the picture on the jigsaw.*

I woke up to Mrs Bolly passed out on my bed and Mr Bolly screaming 'Sweep it under the carpet, sweep it under the carpet.' (*Drops jigsaw piece.*) 'Sweep it under the carpet.' Baffled by the whole affair, I pulled the covers over my head and woke up the next morning under an Axminster. Now you see, Now you see, Now you see.

> *Turns to jigsaw piece, taking hold of it. To the music of Handel's 'Messiah' ('Breaking the Bonds Asunder') she tries rubbing the colour off the jigsaw and off herself. She struggles in a frenzy. While speaking and pointing to the audience her hand posture changes, and she contorts her hand into her imaginary friend Lizard. She stands, still rubbing at her skin, and calls for Lizard, and becomes angry with him as if she's telling him to stop.*

What do you think Lizard?
One banana, two banana, three banana, four,
Five banana, six banana, seven banana, more.

> *Lights dim.* REGINA *moves in stylized chimpanzee movement. Lights slowly come up and she makes the transition into a sophisticated aristobrat. She plays at being an adult.*

Mr Bolly says I de-de-scend from the apes. He says if I go to the zoo I'll see lots of animals who look like me. Mrs Bolly says I'm different, I'm not like the rest. I think she means the chimpanzees at the zoo.

> REGINA *makes chimp noises, moving in chimp style off the throne. When she begins to speak, she falls back into an eight-year-old's voice.*

Lizard, Lizard, stop it
Lizard, Lizard, Lizard,
What do you think Lizard?
Odd girl out

Just remember to shout
I am shouting Lizard I am I am

(*Sings.*) '*There's a brown girl in the ring*', etc.

I look like the alien
From Mars Mars Mars

Hey Lizard let's play
I want to play, let's play
Tell me when to stop

> *Puts her index fingers together and slowly begins to separate them. Suddenly stops, freezes, and makes eye contact with the white members of the audience.*

Ding dong, ding dong,
Your nose is this long.

> *She continues to play and runs back to the throne jumping up and down on it as if it were a trampoline.*

(*Sings.*) '*There's a brown girl in the ring*', etc.

I look like the golly
On the jam jar jar jar

> *Bends head back and raises hands in front of eyes, contorting fingers into an irregular shape. Begins speaking to her imaginary friend.*

My mummy says I can't be Snow White, or Sleeping Beauty but I can
  be the Big Bad Wolf or The Ugly Duckling.
What do you think Lizard?
All black girls
Have got the best curls
But I'm not black, Lizard, I'm not, I'm not
My mummy says I'm coloured, so there
She says I'm coffee coloured
Just like Nescafé
She said I was special
So there
Coz coz Santa brought me down
The chimney on Christmas day.

My mummy said when I was a baby,
I ate all the carrot tops,
Which made my hair go curly, wurly, wurly
My mummy named me after the Queen, she did, she did, she did
She wants me to walk like her,
Talk like her,
Live like her,
I am the Queen
I am I am I am

(*Sings.*) *'There's a brown girl in the ring'*, etc.

I look like the mould
In the cheese, cheese, cheese.

Sweep it under the carpet.

>   *Sits on throne.*

Now you see I descend from a royal sewage of Gorgonzolas. Oh indeed they remained very strong, until they were mistaken for gorillas.

Sweep it under the carpet.

My blue blood comes from a erroneous lineage of Cheddars, a, a, a, Bries, a, a, a, Stiltons, a, a, a, Cambozolas and that was the last we heard of the Gorgonzolas.

Sweep it under the carpet.

>   *Sweeps her body over the throne until she is upside-down.*

Indeed I am the only sane, surviving member of the Royal Family. Sweep it under the carpet. I was found, conducting on the number 69 bus. Sweep it under the carpet. While rapping the National Anthem. (*Stands.*) Oh indeed, it was the same year that poor Prince Charlie was incarcerated at Broadmoor, after being spotted naked stalking my bus, waving the crown jewels above his head, screaming 'Long live the Queen! Long live the Queen! Long live the Queen'. He never ever recovered from the death of the Royal Family, who died after expectorating LSD, sent by well-wishers of course, while meeting on the eve of the millenium at Windsor Castle, to discuss the future of the monarchy.

Sweep it under the carpet.

> *Sits on the throne*

(*Sings.*) *There's a brown girl in the ring*, etc.

I look like the brown
On the tin foil foil foil

Sweep it under the carpet.

Indeed one month of shitting on the throne, has left me penniless.

> *Walks to backdrop of family picture. Becomes distressed and clings on to it while speaking.*

Descendants of my Great, Great, Gran Dadada have sprung up like weeds. Letters from Africa are requesting mobile phones, BMWs, Nike shoes, Ray Bans, Kentucky Fried Chicken, weave ons and S curls. My four sons have caused a major embarrassment, by impregnating the Heinekens, Tennants and Carlsbergs with their 'Sperms'. Their children have been given the title 'The Special Brews of London'. I've had no choice but to set up a trust, Her Majesty's Posse, for the welfare of their 'Seeds'.

Sweep it under the carpet.

> *Turns from picture.*

Indeed my dear brother Laurent Perrier Chandon has saved the day by inspiring the popularity of the church. He has introduced rizlas as the body of Christ, and brandy as the blood of Christ. Now you see I am the Queen, descending from a royal lineage of Africans, a, a, a, Palm Oils, a, a, a, Moët et Chandon's, a, a, a, Cassava Leaves, a, a, a, Gorgonzolas, a, a, a, Maggi Sauces, a, a, a, Special Brews, and that was the very, very, very, last we heard of the natives.

Sweep it under the carpet.

> *Sweeps petticoats over her face.*

Now where was I?
Hello, Hello, Hello, Hello

> *Laughs. Curtsies to whole of the audience and moves in a hypnotic manner. Her speech is a little slurred as if under the influence of sedatives.*

My shrink says I need an electric shock

Reveals her face.

I took stock
My shrink says all negroes are manic
I didn't panic
My shrink says I should be grateful
I was resentful
My shrink says I've got a chip on my shoulder
I began to smoulder
My shrink says I need a rest
I failed his test
My shrink says I am depressed
I was distressed
My shrink says I should be grateful
I was disgraceful
My shrink says I need education
I asked for segregation
My shrink says all negroes are aggressive
I let him live
My shrink says I've got marijuana psychosis
I smoked his prognosis
My shrink says negroes just don't seem to have brains
I didn't complain
My shrink says I belong in the gutter
I began to mutter
My shrink says I'll end up scrubbing floors
I didn't speak any more
My shrink says I shouldn't be seen
I reminded him I am the Queen

Becomes quite child-like, begins to act out of character, looking under the throne, behind it, in front of it.

Sweep it under the carpet.
Sweep it under the carpet.
What do you think Lizard?

Mimes words as she speaks.

I think
Your shrink
Stinks

(*Child's voice.*) Sweep him under the carpet, Regina.

> *Taking hold of her nose, she runs back to the throne, crawling underneath it.*

(*Sings.*) 'There's a brown girl in the ring', etc.

I look like the patient
Behind bars, bars, bars.

Now you see,
My shrink says,
I need pills,
I pushed him off the hill.

> *She crawls from beneath the throne and rolls down the red carpet into the audience, screaming:*

Sweep it under the carpet.
Sweep it under the carpet.
Sweep it under the carpet.

> *'Für Elise' begins to play.*
> *On tiptoe* REGINA *takes a ballet pose and dances back to the throne. She takes her place in the family picture. She becomes part of the family heirloom.*
> *Lights fade to black out.*

BLACK TABOOS

DUMB STRUCK

At times my
black mothers
black fathers
have oppressed me
leaving me
dumbstruck

At times my
black sisters
black brothers
have oppressed me
leaving me dumbstruck.

I'm not quite sure what is more painful, a black person insulting another black person about their skin colour, or a white person insulting us about our skin colour.

I am a dark-skinned black woman who has been cajoled about her skin colour from both black and white people. Names have ranged from 'tar baby' to 'ace of spades' to 'Teflon'. I passed as a small islander from St Kitts for years through fear of other Caribbean people discovering I was first generation African, born in Britain. I didn't want to be bombarded with more insults. Living in London during my teens, I soon learnt that Africans and Caribbeans could dislike each other, and that black could range from being called crocodile skin, to red skin, to non-stick Teflon.

The blacker you were the uglier you were. I was under no illusion that we couldn't hurt each other.

MY SKIN

My skin is my crime
It is my insanity,
My fantasy
My dream

My skin is my trial
It is black
Sometimes oiled
Sometimes ashen

My skin is my sentence
It is with me every day
This reality blocks
My lonesome way

My skin is my custody
It tortures me
Harbours me
And belongs to me

My skin is my cell
It has four limbs
A torso and a head
It has no love and is unfed

My skin is my prison
It enslaves me
Restricts me
And confines me

My skin is my gaoler
My being
My self
My broken pride

My skin is my time
My burden
My tears
My fears

The effect of slavery has helped to cause some of these cancerous rifts between those of us from the African Diaspora. Africans living in Africa often feeling superior to the Africans who were taken as slaves and placed in the Caribbean. Africans in the Caribbean no longer identifying as African and feeling that they are more civilised than their ancestors in Africa.

And Africans from both these geographical places, feeling superior to the black people born and raised in Britain, who have become too English in their eyes. The hardship of coming to work in England during the 50s and 60s, and the difficulties of finding a home to live in, must have been soul destroying.

Not enough money to stay at home and look after their children meant that parents and offspring were separated. Some back home, others farmed out to white foster families, and some abandoned by their black parents.

The issue of physical abuse and domestic violence has also been prevalent among our communities. Some people argue we learnt to beat our children, sexually abuse young people, and rape our women, from the white people who enslaved us. Learnt from our slave masters or not, such violence has also been one of the causes of fragmenting the black family in Britain today.

PLEASE GOD

She felt that long thin leather strap for the eighth time across her dark skin. It sank deep, driving thin bulging weals into her wrist. With brain control, body tense and teeth clenched, Cherry hesitantly stretched out her other arm.

Swish, Swish, Swish, both wrists were red with fury.

Cherry shyly looked up and saw a woman who vaguely resembled herself. 'That will teach you for playing with those Jamaican girls,' the woman spat out. Cherry was confused, this woman was black, she herself was black and the Jamaican girls were too. Her dry eyes wrenched, sketching this woman, observing every movement she made. She cowered into her room, clambered into bed, and cuddled up to the cold stark walls. 'Please God take me away, Please God take me back, Please God,' she prayed.

She escaped with the fairies, falling into her usual frenzied slumber, waking to another Saturday. Cherry hated this day, it began with a bath. She absolutely hated sharing three baths and one shower between six blocks of flats, they reminded her of public urinals.

Cherry queued behind her mother, holding a bucket filled with a loofah, scrubbing brush, Dettol, soap, and Vim. It was her job to scrub the bath pristine clean, fill the bath with hot steaming water and a splash of Dettol, while her mother stood nagging behind her.

'She .... always gets in the bath first,' her mind screamed.

Cherry watched her mother with great detail.

'Her breasts are so huge,' Cherry's mind echoed.

She was disturbed by their gentle sway, shuddering every time she caught a glimpse of the brutal proof of her birth. It seem to resonate with the scars of white savagery that her mother, grandmother and many other women had experienced through slavery.

'How could this woman ever forget me?' she asked the fairies.

Cherry's new friends couldn't answer, they just hovered above keeping watch over her.

'But her tummy is a collage of thousands of dried prunes,' she protested.

The fairies took hold of her hand and lead Cherry into the bath.

She gritted her teeth and gingerly stepped into the warm scummy water. Her intense thoughts always made her forget the routine. Every Saturday she felt the same strong hand push her violently down and the same stern voice reverberate in her ear: 'Stop you nasty English girl, don't bring your filthy habits here,' her mother exclaimed, ramming a wet flannel between her legs.

Somehow the routine, orders, and nagging seemed to disappear with the pungent smell of disinfectants, while she half concentrated on scrubbing her skin and brushing her teeth in the correct African way.

Away with the fairies, chattering with them profusely, she decided it was far more civilised washing in a bath tub, than having to stand in a plastic bowl and wash like she did every day before going to school. And the fairies agreed, assuring her that Saturdays weren't that bad after all.

Bath time over, her mother had finished drying herself and oiling her skin, it was her turn now. She was confused, why should she know that she must grease her skin every day, grease was always used for cooking or for bicycle repairs. 'Shush,' the fairies pleaded.

As she rubbed cocoa butter into her skin, the sweet smell seduced her away from her mother's sharp tones. Instead she amusingly wondered how many wooden spoons this woman would break on her body today. It was one of her private jokes with the fairies. She almost burst out laughing as she remembered the day her mother thought she was Cassius Clay.

She started jumping up and down like a boxer, the fairies pulled Cherry out of the way, and her mother smashed the wall. The look on her mother's face was worth all the wooden spoons and the beatings which came flying after.

'I hate weekends,' Cherry sighed.

She hurriedly dressed, it was the market, cooking and washing next on the agenda. Once at the market she remembered the fun, hustle, bustle, colours, noise and so many different languages and accents for her to absorb. It made her momentarily forget lessons in the kitchen, once home.

She took her position in the kitchen and watched her mother cook, slowly becoming drunk from the spiced aromas. Onions always got her into trouble. Her mother shouted, 'African girls don't cry when their mothers peel onions,' and before she could hear the fairies whispering, 'Well this one does,' a wooden spoon came crashing down on her cheek. If Cherry was left alone for more than two minutes something was destined to go wrong. She would turn the fire up too high, catch the rice, or drip the soup all over the cooker. Cherry blamed the fairies, but decided to keep this secret to herself. She was fascinated by the peculiar foods which, once cooked, were placed on one communal plate and eaten with hands.

Washing clothes was no easier, she rubbed them the English way, wrung the wrong way, and left the soap caked in, she did try but her Englishness seem to cause combustion.

Cherry wished the weekend away, willing Monday to arrive. She loved school, it was a place where she could run riot and let off steam. The bell for home time was always an anticlimax, but the fairies lured her back. They played chase, I-Spy and sang many songs on the way home.

House work, home work, and then the dreaded wait. Her heart jumped every time she heard the footsteps, step, step, step. Cherry ran from the front room to the kitchen, to the bedrooms, to the kitchen, to the front room, checking everything was clean and tidy, even she was pleased with her work tonight, and the fairies were too. But this evening was different, a social worker had come to visit Cherry and see how she was settling in. She followed her mother's instructions, she smiled charmingly and told her how happy she was. The social worker left looking satisfied.

The key turned, and Cherry's thoughts stopped, she froze to attention, and broke into a nervous smile when her mother came into full view.

'What are you smiling for?' her mother asked.

'Nothing,' Cherry replied.

'What do you mean nothing?' her mother quizzed.

'I don't know,' Cherry jittered.

'What did you say to the social worker?' her mother pried.

'Nothing, I don't know, I can't remember,' Cherry stuttered.

'You're lying,' – smash. 'Don't try to defend yourself,' – smash.

'How dare you give that typical British smile?' her mother sneered.

Bang! The door was shut, and Cherry was pushed to the floor, this woman whom she feared spat in her face, rubbed her face into the carpet, and stamped all over her head.

'I'll teach you with your English ways, strip!' her mother enforced. Cherry awkwardly stripped.

'Bend,' her mother instructed, and Cherry bent like a robot. Slash across the back of the knees. If she bent her knees another whip would come. Helpless, she still tried to stop this horrid nightmare, what could she do? She hadn't peeped a word to the social worker. She knew it was the last time she would be seeing her.

When her mother left the room she automatically slackened her legs, and Cherry's mind floated, while the fairies seem to distract her mind from the pain. They suddenly whispered, 'Your mummy is trying to beat the English out of you, the English which was beaten into her mother's ancestors who were brought to Freetown as free slaves. She's trying to beat your white attitudes, white mannerisms, white values, and white smiles from beneath your black ashen skin.'

'But she wants me to keep my English language and posh accent,' Cherry almost cried out aloud to the fairies. They encircled her making beautiful shapes and patterns before her eyes.

She wanted to leave, she wanted God to take her away from this awful place. Cherry begged her friends to tell God of her plan. She never wanted to go home to this strange woman who turned up one day when she was ten, and started taking her away for weekends from the children's home. A year later she was living at home.

'Please God take me away,' Cherry whispered before collapsing in a heap. She began to hear strange noises, garbled words, it wasn't Creole or Mende. Who was her mother talking to? And then she heard the phone being slammed down.

Cherry listened intently, she heard murmurs and sobs from the front room. 'Please God what have I done to deserve this? What have I done to deserve this child?' Her mother wailed and broke down and cried. 'Please God forgive me,' her mother spluttered. For one moment Cherry and the fairies felt sorry for this woman, and then she crawled into bed trembling, turned over, placed her head beneath the pillow and silently cried too. 'Please God.'

SECTION FIVE

CONFUSED? CELEBATE? LESBIAN?

THE ANTONIAN SEA

Ripples are running across her big broad back,
Flowing all over her body,
Gentle waves, ebbing and easing the stress away.

Silver, all shades of Blues,
Spread across her voluptuous body.

She whispers, She sighs, She moans,
Sometimes screeching in harmony,
With the breath of the winds.

I try to reach beneath her blue silvery skin,
Caress her serene beauty,
Watch her tranquilly bob up and down.
I try to look beyond her boundaries,
Her curves, her movement, engulf my vision.

I can see as far as the sky meets the sea,
And the sea meets the sky.
She continues to pass me by.. and by.. and by..

Blowing the odd kiss,
Pushing her tiny waves into the sand.

I am left with her smells, salt, sand, seaweed,
On my fingertips, in my hair, in my blood,
Soaked into every pore of my body.

Barcelona – Spring 1990

THE CLAUDE

Her rugged mane,
Ripples,
Swishes,
Spurts,
Foaming from her mouth, her troubles.

She is serene,
Like the crystals in the earth.
Her transparency glistens,
All Day,
Noon,
And Night.

Tainted ripples,
Tiny humps,
White foam,
Blur the contour of her body,
Her clarity masks the complexities of her body.

Rough edges,
Jagged rocks,
Matted seaweed,
Are littered along the base of her seabed.

Choppy waves,
A placated surf,
The odd ferocious storm,
Are proof of her tiresome life.

Her pain,
Her strength,
Her pleasures,
Are the minerals of the waters.

She washes away the pain,
Rinses away the stress,
Drains away the anger of other oceans too.

The Claude is laced with joy,
With sadness,
With wisdom,
Her salts rejuvenate,
Replacing the equilibrium of calm.

The Claude stretches beyond my perimeter,
Beneath my walls,
The Claude links up to another bay in my mind.

Mykonos – Summer 1991

THE ALEX – PART I

Some months ago I woke up lost on her shores.

Although her rocks, pebbles, and shells,
Seemed familiar,
Her tar was of a new strange brand.

As I tried to stand,
Her damp sand glued me to her beach,
I was stuck to her drift wood,
And bound by her seaweed.

The Alex laughed,
She groaned.
Crashing her huge waves all over my body.

Foaming and spraying her juices,
Drenching me with her waters,
Saturating me with her minerals,
Embracing me with her waves.

My body jerked from her seabed,
Releasing itself from the mesh of seaweed chains.
I spluttered and splashed,
Doggy paddled in new waters.

Until I allowed myself to be
Tossed by her gentle gale,
Thrown by the wrath of her storm

Thrown by the wrath of her storm

Thrown by the wrath of her storm

I am floating, floating, floating.

Paris – Autumn 1991

THE ALEX – PART II

I am shipwrecked
Marooned
Washed up on her shore.

Abandoned
Deserted
Stranded.

Her huge storm engulfs me
The sand beneath my feet is
Shifting, shifting, shifting.

Swept off my feet by her ferocious rip.

Dumped
Beachcombed
Fossilised.

Submerged in new waters
My heart is
Drifting, drifting, drifting

Cast out to sea by her tempest.

I am coasting, coasting, coasting.

Kefalonia – Summer 1992

THE GITANJALI

Her beauty glistens in her sands,
Sparkling bright jewels
Twinkling all over her beach.

She is a sea of dolphins,
Diving from cliff to cliff.

Her beauty ripples in her oceans
Big waves dancing to and fro,
Splashing all over her beach.

She is a sea of seaweed,
Gyrating from bay to bay.

Her beauty rainbows on every shell
Frolicking all over her seabed
Tumbling up and down

She is a sea of blossoming life,
Thunderstorming from sky to sky.

Berlin – Winter 1993

THE FANTASY

I can feel her rollicking waves,
Rippling up my spine,
Splashing each vertebra,
Spraying every cartilage and muscle.

I can feel her rapid storms,
Resonating from head to toe,
Tumbling each cell,
Tossing every vein.

She pulsates, morning, day and night,
Surging all over her soft sandy shores.

Moaning at five,
Roaring at six,
Sighing at seven,
Screeching at eight,
Overflowing at nine.

Her undercurrent changes each second,
Her tides every minute.

She is impermanent like her wet billowy winds,
Whirling each thought,
Fluxing every sensation.

For one moment I ride,
With her,
On white galloping horses,
The next ...
I watch another ride too.

She plays,
She storms,
She breaks,
Surfing each body,
Beachcombing every limb.

Shropshire – Winter 1994

It's Winter 1998, and I'm single and many of my friends are too. I can still hear the adults, at the dinner table sharing their anecdotes: 'If you reach twenty-five and you're not married you're on the shelf,' Aunty Hazel often said. I once actually tried sitting on the shelf and she told me off for breaking the vases. Perhaps you can add another ten years on in the lesbian community, which gives me some hope, otherwise I'm long past the sell-by date.

The scene has changed, one night stands seem harder to negotiate, and some women are turning to the classifieds to maintain their promiscuous life, or find a wife. The fact is, we are all getting older.

It's 7 am, March 8th 1998, and I'm sitting under a railway arch, hard core techno is blasting. I've danced my socks off with women I've got wrecked with for years. It's Lu's birthday, and we're celebrating her big Four-O. Strange that, she's the first of the women I've grown up with on the scene to make it, and one by one during the next eight years each of us will turn forty.

It still seems the same as fifteen years ago, all of us out raving on the scene. None of us seems to have changed. But the scene is different, ten years ago Lu's celebration would have been women only, no men allowed. Women only seems passé nowadays, most of our bars in London allow men in as guests.

I'm not sure what it means to be a lesbian anymore. In fact I'm not sure what it meant fifteen years ago, apart from the fact that there were clear rules to live by, and I went along with the ones that suited me without thinking for myself.

Today some of the women I've grown up with are transgendering, living as men in the world, and there are lesbians who are happily dating them. And my lesbian separatist politics are slowly melting away and the rules seem more flexible, even though it's harder to know where you stand.

I was once asked in an interview if I would go out with a female-to-male (F-to-M) transgender by an interviewer who was an F-to-M transgender person. I didn't have the courage to say I've been having sexual fantasies about this. But fantasies are safe, and it still wouldn't have answered the question. I suppose the answer is No, as I'm still very attached to the labels 'lesbian' and 'dyke', and to sexually relate to an F-to-M would for me challenge these comfortable identities.

Once upon a time I was at the same conference with lesbians who are now living as men. All of us were affected by the lesbian separatist thought police during the early 1980s, who organised conferences and stated we couldn't penetrate our lovers, because we would be acting out heterosexuality, and colluding with patriarchy, by making the woman the victim.

Several years later, while working in Australia, I end up in bed with a woman who is able to swallow my whole hand up her vagina. I panic, I remember my beloved sisters lecturing 'fist fucking equals abuse', 'penetration equals victim'. But they didn't warn me about the women who could just open up to the size of a football.

During 1983 a Lesbians and Sexual Practice conference took place in London, and some radical lesbian separatist feminist claimed that dildos and sex toys were in the same jamboree bag as sado-masochistic sexual practices, without listening to the issues concerning this sexuality. Today I'm faced with lesbians wanting dicks, rubber ones, real ones and pretend ones.

Fifteen years later, girls with dicks have become acceptable, perhaps through the advent of 'queer' in 1991, which encouraged men and women to play with gender: anyone who actively challenged the sexual and gender norms could be queer, including heterosexuals.

This gave some lesbians the permission to go out packing with a strap-on dildo and pick up gay men 'giving them one up the arse', and still define themselves as lesbians.

Packing went one step further for some women, dragging up as men for fun and sex, and some pushed the boundaries even further by transgendering. The lesbian separatist thought police seem to have been in a deep sleep. Help! Now we have to think for ourselves.

Some of us are perhaps too frightened to comment on trans-gendering, others not wanting to pass judgement on women we've hung out with on the scene for years, and how many of us really understand what it means to transgender if we haven't done it ourselves?

While lesbian transgendering is about changing one's gender and queer is about a specific type of bisexuality, these lifestyle choices have not received the vociferous attacks that lesbian sado-masochism has. S and M is still in the margins of the British lesbian community. Little has changed since the late 1980s when the lesbian thought police came out armed with crowbars and tried to demolish the first openly public lesbian S and M club, Chain Reaction, in London: the only city in Britain which has got away with such a venue.

Suzie Krueger's Clit Club during the early 1990s provided a safe place for girls to bring the antics of their private parties (the famous East End gatherings) into the public domain of a night club. In 1998 a lesbian S and M play-space, 'Endorfine', is held once a month at the gay male club Central Station, playing host to twenty or so who talk about sex and play with chains, slings and a St Andrew's cross. Its word of mouth publicity is perhaps proof of the taboo, or the hang-over, of a lesbian separatist politic.

Growing up with all this around me has allowed me to be single and promiscuous, being more open and alive to, and (hopefully) more honest and articulate, about my confusions.

I've always since my awakening been a dyke (up front lesbian with global politics and in yer face attitude), always had sexual relation-ships with women, always been attracted to women, but sometimes I feel as if I want to let go of my attachment to dykedom, bury my head under the pillow, become a Buddhist nun and lead a spiritual life. My friends laugh of course, wouldn't you? Being so attached to my lesbian self, black self, female self, has slowly come to feel a hindrance to my personal growth. While these identities have allowed me to grow and heal they now feel confining; though a part of me but not the total sum of me, I am bigger than all these identities.

THE PERSONAE

I am a crescendo of waves,
Plunging all over your pebbled beach.
I am a cascading storm,
Flooding all over your muddy shores.

My tide flows towards authentic love
My tide pulls towards authentic friendship

My impermanent waves
Seduce the vulnerable,
Entice the invincible.

My storms embrace my prey,
Greeting you with
Ripples of Silver,
Greys,
Greens,
Blues,
Browns,
Blacks.

I am personified in every Raindrop.
In every Pond.
In every Canal.
In every River.
In every Lake.
In every Ocean.

Loch Eck by Dunoon – 1997